LT OVER THE EDGE

ER THE

EDGE

Tackling Quarterbacks, Drugs,

Lawrence Taylor
with Steve Serby

and a World Beyond Football

HarperCollins*Publishers*

HarperCollins books may be purchased for educational, business, or sales promotional use. For information, please write: Special Markets Department, HarperCollins Publishers Inc., 10 East 53rd Street, New York, NY 10022.

FIRST EDITION

Designed by Elliott Beard

Printed on acid-free paper

Library of Congress Cataloging-in-Publication Data is available upon request.

ISBN 0-06-018551-1

04 05 06 07 08 ❖/RRD 10 9 8 7 6 5 4 3 2 1

ACKNOWLEDGMENTS AND THANKS

I have so many people to thank for standing by me, for supporting me, for guiding me, for rooting for me every step of the way: my parents; my children; my brothers; Paul Davis; D'Fellas; Vicki; Gary Gaglioti; Dino; Wellington Mara; the late George Young; Bill Parcells; George Martin; Harry Carson; Eric Hayes; Charlie Stucky and everyone at Honesty House; my current wife, Maritza.

And to my ex-wife, Linda, who lived through a nightmare, and always tried to help: I apologize for everything I put you through.

Lawrence Taylor

AUTHOR'S NOTE

That's what they call these things, right? "Author's Note"? I'm not really sure about that, because I don't read a lot of books, unless they're ones I wrote, of course. Well, whatever you want to call this section, I wanted to explain the ground rules for this book up front. First off, this is my autobiography, which you probably already know if you read the cover. But there are a few things you may not know. The first is that I've already written an autobiography. It was called *LT: Living on the Edge*. It came out about sixteen years ago. I thought it was a pretty good book, and I was proud of it. But there was a big problem with that book. It didn't tell the best part of my story. And the worst.

You see, in my first book, I talked about my triumphs on the field, then my slide into hell with cocaine addiction, and my "triumphant" recovery. Well, guess what? That recovery was only a speed bump on my ride toward a crack binge that almost took my family, my reputation, and my life.

But I pulled out of it. With the love and guidance of a lot

of people, that is. And since I got a second chance in my life, I figured I deserved a second chance with my autobiography. Because I've got a better story to tell this time. And since it's my book, I'm telling it my way. So I've asked a lot of friends and family to add their memories of the good times. And the bad times. And there were plenty of both. I know an autobiography's supposed to be written by "the guy," but I was always a team player on the football field, so why not call on my "teammates" now?

Besides, they remember a lot of things I can't, or don't want to remember. And I've always said, if you can remember everything you did last night, you weren't having enough fun.

PROLOGUE NO SUPERMAN HERE

Sonuvabitch put a gun to my head. I thought I was dead.
I was cruising through a nasty-ass place in Spring Valley, New York, called The Hill. It was late. Real late. But I wanted some cocaine. I needed some cocaine.

My name is Lawrence Taylor and I'm an addict . . . and addicts don't care if they have to venture into dangerous hellholes like The Hill if there's a pot of cocaine at the end of the rainbow.

I saw three guys who looked like they were carrying, and I knew I was in business. They were all young black dudes, but I couldn't tell you nothing else about them. In a situation like that, you don't go looking at faces. I didn't pay no attention to what they were wearing. I wasn't there to make friends.

I pulled over in my Cadillac, and one guy got in my front seat and one guy got in the backseat. I didn't like that, so I said, "Yo, I don't want two guys in my car." But the guy standing outside pulled out some shit, so I bought it.

After we had done our business, I noticed that the guy in

the front seat was looking hard at my big gold Rolex, the one with diamonds. The dude asked me, "Is that real?" I started to have a bad feeling about the way this conversation was going, so I said, "Y'all have to get out of my car. Let's go, get outta here."

The guy in the backseat got out and closed the door. The guy in the front seat made like he was getting out, but then he got back in, turned toward me, and stuck a gun in my face. "Gimme the watch, motherfucker."

I said, "*Noooooo* problem, bro. Just don't shoot."

I was scared. Shit yes. I took my watch off and gave it to him. Little did he know that I had about $10,000 cash in my pocket; I carried a lot of money in those days—you never know when a poker game's going to break out. He put the watch on the seat between us, and then said he wanted my diamond pinkie ring. He didn't ask me to take it off, he just started tugging on it. He 'bout tore my finger off trying to get that sonuvabitch off. I was like, "Hey, man, I'll get it off myself, okay?"

I handed him the ring, and he handed his gun to the guy standing outside the car, and told him to get in. Now I realized they're about to jack me, take my car. The guy with the gun pulled on the back door, but the door was locked—thank God for those annoying safety features on expensive cars—so his pal in the front seat had to reach over the seat to unlock the door. So now his body's between me and the guy with the gun. I see my opening. My chance.

I slammed the Caddy into drive, and stomped on the gas. I banged over the curb, swerving like a crazy man, and the guy sitting next to me was screaming, "Stop, motherfucker! I'm going to kill you!"

I was throwing that car from side to side, trying to throw him back and forth so he can't shoot me. We go about two hundred yards before I remember this punk ain't got no gun. He gave it to the other guy, right? So I screeched to a stop and started pounding him in the face with my fists. I wasn't scared now. "Where's my shit?" *Bam!* "Gimme my shit!" *Bam! Bam!*

Needless to say, he was suddenly more than happy to give me my watch and ring back. After he handed them over, though, I looked through my back window and saw that the other two guys—the guy with the gun and the dude who was in the backseat—were running down the street, coming right for us. And they were *comin'*, too, boy. So I yelled at the guy in my passenger seat, "Get out!" But he just sat there, moanin' like a bitch, his hands covering his bloody face, so I reached across him, opened the door, and yelled, "Get out!" He still didn't move, so I hit the gas. Meanwhile, his buddies were closing on us. The front passenger door is still open, so I grab that punk ass by the neck and shove him out of the car.

And then I drove home and smoked their crack.

I never saw them again, but the guy I threw out of the car must have gone to jail for doing something else to somebody else, because I found out six months later that I had broken the guy's jaw. A friend of mine who had done some time said someone in there had been bragging to people about jacking LT. Stupid motherfucker.

That wasn't my only brush with death. Just my closest.

That night on The Hill was in the midnineties, during a

period when the only people in my life were dealers, addicts, and hookers. My life was in serious turmoil, and I was chasing cocaine the way I used to chase quarterbacks—with relentless, reckless abandon. I wasn't just living in the fast lane—hell, I was dyin' in it.

How could this have happened to me? I mean, I was the great Lawrence Taylor! LT! Superman in Giant blue. The greatest defensive player, maybe, in NFL history. Every quarterback's worst nightmare.

And now I was a desperate loser begging for mercy from punk thieves. My glory days seemed like an eternity ago.

CHAPTER ONE

CLARENCE, my dad

LT was what you saw on the field playing for the Giants, but at home he was Lonnie. Lonnie was aggressive but lovable. He would do anything for you. Very polite. LT was very aggressive. Wanted to be known as a rough, tough kinda guy. Take-your-head-off kind. In your face.

IRIS, my mom

He was a challenging child. Where the other two boys would ask for permission to do stuff, Lonnie—his family and friends, we always call him Lonnie—would just do it, and when you found out about it, he would give you a big story.

Growing up in Williamsburg, Virginia, I always had respect for my mom and dad. I had perfect attendance every year in school, and I was a decent student. When I applied myself, which wasn't all that often. I wasn't what you would call a Goody Two-shoes. Even as a youngster I had a problem with curfews.

IRIS

I didn't let my children roam the streets. All our boys had curfews. They would come in and say good night and then go to bed. But then Lonnie would go out the window and go to a party. See, I had spies all over Williamsburg and everybody knew my children. One of them told me one time, "I saw your son at a party last night," and I said, "No, it couldn't have been. My sons are home at twelve."

She said, "I don't know exactly which one it was, but he was having a good old time." So I said, "Hmmmm."

I'd normally wake up at three o'clock in the morning and I would go in and do a bed check. I always wanted to be sure my kids were safe. Lonnie must have known that, so he'd come home before three. So I got up at two and went into the bedroom to do my check, and that little rascal was gone! So I waited for him. After a while, he knocked on the window, and I hear him whisper to his brother, "Kim, Kim, open the door."

I said, "That's all right, Kim, I got it!" I unlocked the door and hid. When Lonnie came in, I grabbed him from behind. I grounded him for a week.

Yeah, I guess you could say I had plenty of mischief in me, and sometimes my parents would need to get my attention with a belt—or a switch from a birch tree. I liked to see what I could get away with.

IRIS

He was good at conning people. He was a smooth talker. He could talk you out of anything.

One time, when I was eleven, I borrowed my dad's bicycle, which I wasn't supposed to do. I figured, Who'd know?

CLARENCE

I bought four bicycles, one for each boy and one for myself. I told them, "These are your bicycles and this is mine. If you break your bicycle you're not getting mine."

I was at work one day and Lawrence borrowed my bicycle and rode downtown. He ran into something and messed it up. He didn't know what to do, so he came back home. I had an old '72 Chevrolet pickup with a manual shift, which he didn't know how to drive that well. He proceeded to get the bicycle, but because he didn't know how to shift gears, he drove it in low gear all the way and messed the transmission up. He got someone with a wrecker to bring my truck back to the house and put it in the same place, and then he wiped out the tracks so I couldn't see that the truck had been moved. He put the bicycle in the trash somewhere, I suppose.

When I went to use the truck the next day, I thought something had just happened to the transmission. Lawrence never said anything about it until years afterward.

So I went from borrowing a bike to destroying it and my dad's pickup. Hmm, I wonder if that was any indication of what the future had in store for me? Anyway, my poor dad thought his bike had been stolen until he read my first book.

My parents had their hands full with three sons. I was in the middle—it was me, Buddy, and Kim. We struggled a bit financially when I was growing up, but I didn't know too many black families back then who didn't struggle some. But I never left the house hungry. Mom and Dad worked hard to bring us up. Dad had a job in the shipyards at Newport News, and Mom worked low-paying jobs at places like the five-and-dime or the Laundromat. We made out better than most. And if I ever needed some spending money, I'd get creative.

BUDDY,
my older brother

One time he stole some jeans from Woolworth's. Then he took them back and told them they were too big and he wanted his money back. He got his money!

I'd also borrow money from my mother, buy candy from Happy's Store, and sell it at school for a profit—sometimes to my brothers. That's why they called me the Candy Man. I'd make out so good I'd lend Mom money so she could go to the movies.

KIM,
my younger brother

One day our mother was in our room and Lonnie, who was thirteen or so at the time, said, "Mom, when I become rich, I'm going to buy you a house."

She said, "You don't even want to go to school, how are you going to become rich?"

He said, "Mark my words." We all laughed.

But big was the only way I knew how to dream. It was something I always did with my friends—D'Fellas. They were my boys and we were tight. Throughout my life, I'd always felt comfortable around them and could just be myself. We would do everything together, even sing. J.D., Cosmo, and Dylan Pritchett were the singers. Eric Stone, Eric Pruden, and myself, we'd throw in our bass 'cause that's all we had. They'd give me one, two lines and that was enough. We'd sing all over, going to the movies or while we were just hanging out.

On summer nights as young teenagers we'd hang by the Old Moorestown Bridge, sometimes with beer, sometimes not, watching the trains go by. We had no worries then, no responsibilities.

ERIC STONE, a D'Fella

We had this old wooden bridge within half a mile of where we lived where we'd all sit at night and talk. We always talked about what we would be doing after high school and college. We all knew he'd end up going to the pros. He never bragged; we did all that for him.

GLENN "COSMO" CARTER, a D'Fella

He was someone who could always foresee the future before it was gonna happen, or knew exactly where he was going. Didn't know how he was gonna get there . . . always a dreamer, I guess.

Every Thanksgiving Day, the whole neighborhood would gather at a field we called the Sunken Gardens for the Turkey Bowl. It was right behind where William and Mary played. It was tackle football, of course. It's about as long as a football field, and you'd have twenty-five or thirty guys on each team. No holds barred. If you could take the heat, come into the kitchen. Those were the days. It started at eleven o'clock and lasted till three, three-thirty. Till you just got tired.

We also loved to play cards. Every Friday night we'd play spades and it'd last for hours and hours and hours.

ERIC PRUDEN, a D'Fella

The games would float from house to house. If he was on your team, he's gonna try to calculate, "Okay, if we're playing to fifty, we gotta score such and such every hand" to make sure we get to fifty before the next team.

He hated to lose. He has a will to win; no matter what we're playing, cards, basketball, marbles, he's gonna try to find a way to win. It was kind of unnerving sometimes. You had to make sure you beat him down—he wasn't gonna concede.

We'd also race cars all around town.

DYLAN PRITCHETT, a D'Fella

We played tag with our cars. He drove a baby-blue Maverick and he had Keystone rims. I had the very same car, the very same year, the very same make and color. Only I had Cragar rims. We would just ride through the streets of Williamsburg trying to lose each other. We'd be zooming down one street, then I'd see his lights and then I'd follow him until I got him cornered. Then he was "it."

We all had nicknames. Pritchett was The Prick, because he bragged that he had a big dick. Cosmo was kinda out there. Eric Stone was Stoney. Eric Pruden was The Doc, because he was always reading books. John J. D. Morning was Hollywood because he was the ladies' man. They called me

The Monster, because I was bigger than the others. Maybe it was also because I always had a high threshold for pain.

KIM

He was always into things. If he could think of it, he would try it. As kids, we used to climb trees and we would see who could climb the highest in the tree. When Lonnie was twelve, I think, he had an idea: he would jump from one tree to another tree. He had seen it in a Tarzan movie. So he jumped, and of course the tree didn't hold him. We heard a big noise—he fell all the way down to the ground. He had cuts and bruises all over him, but he gets up, wipes himself off, and tries it again.

I must've gotten my toughness from my dad. He had been a boxer; I think he went to the Golden Gloves. And he played for the local softball team, the Toano (Virginia) Giants. He was raised by his grandmother and was working full-time by the time he was nineteen. He was twenty when he married Mom (who was eighteen). Dad wasn't a big guy, but he would join me and my brothers for some two-on-two hoops in the backyard, and sometimes it was me and him, one-on-one. We played a little bit of football, too.

CLARENCE

The boys would wait for me to come home from work so they could play two-on-two football—sometimes touch, sometimes tackle—in the backyard. They would meet me in our driveway with the ball. Lawrence was nine or ten at the time, but he would tackle me. He liked the challenge of it. As he got to eleven, twelve, thirteen, I had to put a little muscle into it. I had to get a little rough with him. He liked the contact.

Growing up, I liked the Cowboys, but I didn't really get into learning football till I started playing, and only on my level. I had never been to a professional football game until I played in one. Dad was a Redskins fan, though. He'd watch high school, college, pros, and my brothers would watch with him more often than I would. Me, I'd rather play.

My dad and I were close when I was growing up, but then, toward the middle years of my childhood, not that close. We've gotten closer again now that I'm older. When I was younger, I didn't understand a lot of the things my dad would do. The arguments he would have with my mom and everything . . . He would go out every Friday and Saturday night, and wouldn't come home till late. I couldn't understand that kind of behavior toward my mother when I was a boy. But as I got older, I got to understand it a little better, because I was doing shit like that myself. It didn't make it right, but my experiences gave me a different perspective.

Dad used to tell me, "You gotta be twice as good as the white man to be equal." That made me want to excel. He encouraged me to play football, even though I felt my best sport was baseball. I was a catcher, and when I hit that sucker, the center fielder wouldn't say, "I got it!" He'd say, "I'll go get it!" My mom didn't want me playing football, because she was afraid I might get hurt, but my dad kept telling her to let me play, and she finally gave in. She was the one who'd take me to Pop Warner games.

I got interested in the football city league when I was about thirteen, but that was only because the team got to take a trip to Pittsburgh every year. That was going just fine until one day a coach, Mel Jones, the running backs' and linebackers' coach, challenged me to come out for the high school team, at Lafayette High.

MEL JONES

First time I saw Lawrence, he was standing against the wall in the commons, probably watching the girls. This was halfway through the football season. I said to him, "Hey man, are you playing football?"

He said, "Yeah, coach, I'm playing."

I said, "You're lying. I'm out there, I don't see you."

He told me he was playing in the peewee league, so I told him, "That don't count. You have to play with the big boys, 'cause they don't give scholarships there in the recreation league."

He said he'd come out his junior year. And I made sure he did. Every time I saw him, I'd remind him, especially when he was walking with a girl. When Lawrence would say he was coming out for football next season, I'd say, "Did you hear that, honey? Make sure he don't lie to me!"

Well, he did come out the next season, but he wasn't

very successful in the beginning. He was playing street ball, but you could see he had raw talent. He played defensive end and tight end, and got bounced around a little bit. Halfway through one of his first practices, he got frustrated. He went in the locker room, and I was right behind him. He said, "The hell with this shit!"

I said, "You made a commitment to play. You've got to honor your commitment. You'll be okay. I ain't going back on that football field without you. You haven't given yourself a chance."

Lawrence said, "No, coach, no!" He was taking his stuff off, so I threatened to tell everybody in school that the kids had run him off. He didn't like that. He put his football gear back on, and went back out to the field.

Football is not a game for the weak of heart, because every day you've got a hundred reasons to take all those pads off and say, "Fuck it." Especially when you're in training camp for the first time and you go through all those drills. There's a hundred reasons why you should just say, "I'm outta here!" But I wasn't raised a quitter.

I was hardly an overnight sensation. I played guard and center on offense and defensive end. I played tight end and defensive end as a senior, and I enjoyed both positions, but I always liked defense best. I knew right away that I'd rather hit than be hit.

MEL JONES

Halfway through that first season, Lawrence began opening eyes. We were playing Bethel High School. He sacked the quarterback and almost knocked him out. He intercepted a pass later and ran it all the way back. I said, "Hmmm. That little kid's coming around, ain't he?"

That happened about five games into my junior year. Bethel was the best team in our district, and on the first play of the second quarter, the defensive end playing in front of me went down, so they threw me into the fray. I was scared shitless at first, but I got over my nerves real quick and ended up having a phenomenal game. I was chasing guys down all over the yard, and I blocked a punt which we recovered for a touchdown and we won 6–0. From that game till the end of my senior year, I got better and better. By the end of my junior year, there was talk of me being all-state, and by the middle of my senior year, I felt I could dictate what went on on the football field.

MEL JONES

Lawrence had grown to around six-foot-one, 207 pounds by his senior year. He was cat quick, and he could catch the football. He was athletically inclined.

Still, he drew little interest from colleges. He didn't have the grades for William and Mary, and it didn't work out with Richmond.

Mel wanted me to play real bad. He called his old school, Norfolk State, and asked them to take a look at me. Dick Price, the head coach, told Mel that he had seen me play against Hampton High.

MEL JONES

Dick told me, "Taylor's a good little player, but he's not that large."

"He'll grow!" I said. "The kid can play football!" Price passed.

Then UNC came. A scout had told Bill Dooley, the head coach, about me, and he came to watch me play basketball.

BILL DOOLEY

I thought to myself, "If this guy can hit anybody . . ." He was unbelievable. He could go up and down the court, jump, move, had quick feet. I met LT just to say a quick hello. Then I told my recruiter to go ahead and get him.

I redshirted LT for his freshman year, but it wasn't long, just two or three games, before I watched LT in practice and wondered if I had made a mistake. We couldn't run against him. I said, "He oughta be on the varsity."

Hey, Bill, I could've told you that!

CHAPTER TWO

AL GROH, now head coach at Virginia, was the linebacker coach at UNC and the Giants

He had an energy level about him that was very apparent, a sparkle in his eye.

We had two outside linebackers, one was a senior, one was a junior, and both of them went on to make All-ACC. That's the only reason LT didn't get significant minutes as a freshman. He just had such obvious talent . . . such explosion. Obviously I had never coached a player that had the explosiveness that Lawrence did. Almost thirty years later, I've probably never coached one like him.

I first made my mark at UNC on special teams. On the punt team, I'd come up the middle and jump over the fullback who was blocking for the kicker. He'd nail me low, and

I'd flip over him and land on my head. Every damn time. I never blocked a punt. Always came close, but I never could block that sonuvabitch. But the coaches loved the effort and the crowd would go, "Woo, woo!"

My sophomore year, I started out at inside linebacker, but in the first quarter of the first game, I cracked my ankle and they moved another linebacker in. The guy playing behind me was an excellent player. I was out for three or four games, and once he got in there, it was hard for me to get back in. So they found someplace else for me to play—nose tackle. Ugh! That was no fun at all. I don't like playing inside, because you're taking on people from everywhere. You got the guard to worry about, you got the center to worry about, you got people coming at you from the right side, you got people coming at you from the left side . . . I did not like that one bit.

My junior year, they put me at outside linebacker. And I wasn't standing out at first, just playing mediocre. It might have been in the fifth game, against NC State, when everything changed. I forced a fumble, recovered it, and took it to the house. That's when the publicity really started. From that game until the end of my college career, I became unstoppable.

That was also a big day because I met Linda Cooley at a local bar called Mayo's. She was a sophomore, and needless to say, I made an impression.

LINDA, my ex-wife

He was a big bully back then. He'd walk through the club all big and bad. If you were in his way, he had a tendency to knock you out of his way. He came toward me one night and I didn't move. I asked him, "Why are you such a bully? Why are you pushing everybody around?" I don't remember what his response was, but from that point on we started hanging out.

He was a charmer. He once told me he wanted to marry me if I was to look anything like my mother.

Back on the field, I realized that I was loving football. I enjoyed the enthusiasm that goes with college football, the spirit, the energy, the sense that every game is do or die.

STEVE STREATER,
my pal and defensive back at UNC

In the Bluebonnet Bowl, Herky Walls, a Texas sprint champ, ran a down-and-out and he broke it loose. I was running after him and Lawrence passed me up and said, "You gotta do better than that" on his way to catching him and saving a touchdown. I said, "Look at this fool!"

LT talked trash, saying things like, "Son, you got to do better than this!" And he'd taunt players from NC State or Clemson with an "I told you you shoulda come to Carolina." Or: "Don't come over this way no more." Or: "You better run the other way."

Schoolwise, I did what I had to do. Somebody once asked me how seriously I took my classes at North Carolina, how

much studying I did. I said, "Look, I'm a football player, not an educator. You don't need four years of French or two years of nuclear physics to knock the shit out of somebody."

By my junior year, people started telling me that I could make it to the pros, and they started calling me Filthy McNasty—I was clean, but mean—and I loved the name. That makes sense, of course, because I had come up with that name myself. I had been looking for a rough-and-tough nickname for a while, something to reflect how I like to play hard—and hit hard. In the Gator Bowl against Michigan my junior year, I was going full tilt.

JOHN WANGLER,
quarterback, Michigan Wolverines

It was like a third-and-long, and we were deep in our own territory, up 9–0. We had a bootleg called to the wide side of the field and Lawrence was the outside linebacker there. We were pulling the backside guard [Kurt Becker] to block Lawrence. There was a corner blitz and I got a little nervous and I didn't give him time to get in front of me, so I ended up getting down the line before [Becker] had a chance to block Lawrence.

I initially tried to beat him to the corner. When I realized I wasn't gonna beat him, I turned up inside on him, and my right leg planted in the ground. I started to go down and I felt something pop, which was my right knee. It hyperextended back.

I had no idea at that time how well Lawrence Taylor could play the game. He did not yet have a national reputation. He could run sideline to sideline; it was ridiculous.

There had been a lot of cheap shots and yapping during the game, and now Lawrence added insult to injury. He rolled me and twisted it a little bit. A lot of people thought it was deliberate, but I couldn't really tell. I was going down. Something snapped before he even got me and rolled me. I never thought it was intentional.

When I was being helped off the field, Lawrence was jumping around and yapping. He was excited that he put me out, believe me.

Lawrence: "Get up! Get up!" [Plus some X-rated extras.]

Wangler: "Hey, don't worry, I'll be back. Look at the scoreboard. I'll be back."

I tore three ligaments, including the posterior cruciate, and some cartilage, and we lost.

About ten years ago, I ran into LT at a banquet in Detroit. He came up and said, "How's your leg?" I said, "It's better than it was that night. Listen, the only thing that made me mad is you got a lot of credit for taking me out. I think I was going down before you got to me." He laughed.

I've never felt good about any player getting hurt, but it was a clean play and my reaction during the game was more because I was jacked up and in the moment. At the time, I didn't know how bad the injury was, especially since quarterbacks are always crying anyway.

Off the field, no one wanted to mess with me, that's for

sure, except for the stupid ones. One night I was playing nine-ball in a bar and making some nice money. One guy finally beats me and he's celebrating with his beer and some splashes on me. "Why'd you do that?" I asked. "Because I felt like it," he said. So while the mutha is racking up the balls for another game, I take my glass of beer and pour it over him. He got all pissed off. "Why did you do that?" he asked. "Because I felt like it," I said. He took a swing at me and then all hell broke loose. We left that bar a wreck.

All the football players stayed in one dormitory, Ehring House. We'd come home from celebrating after a big win and someone would say, "Hey! We didn't get in a fight tonight." So we'd hop in a car, go to a bar, get into a fight, and come back home. Saturday-night fighting was a big thing.

BUDDY

Lonnie got away with plenty in college. The policemen at Chapel Hill never bothered him. Lonnie told me a judge told the cops one time, "If y'all bring a football player in front of me, I'm going to let him go."

STEVE STREATER

One time we went uptown; we had us a couple of cold ones. It doesn't snow that much in Chapel Hill and this day we got a nice little snow. Everybody got into a snowball fight. LT threw a snowball so hard it knocked a car window out, so we took off running back to the dorm. We got back, we started a snowball fight with the dorm across the street from us. He threw a snowball and knocked a guy out.

I'd also do some stupid things that would just build up my reputation, like climb up the face of Ehring House, usually while I was blind drunk. I'd scale the six stories and people would look at me like, well, like I was Superman.

RICKY BARDEN played defensive back at UNC

At that time, the dormitory had these elevators that had a window in the middle of the elevator. LT was bored. He just said, "I feel like hitting somebody." And he took his fist and broke through the glass. We were looking at the blood on his arm and he's like, "It's no big deal. I'll be ready to play."

DONNELL THOMPSON
played defensive tackle at UNC

Lawrence had a short fuse. Pity anyone who yelled something derogatory about the Tarheels while Lawrence was walking down Franklin Street. Lawrence would run to the car and chase the guy down and whip his ass.

Then there was the time during a pool game at Mayo's when I looked up and saw Lawrence take a bite out of a glass and start chewing it. I'm like, "You're out of your mind!"

Our goal-line stand against Clemson my senior year was one of the greatest goal-line stands I have ever seen. They had four downs to go one yard and we wouldn't let them into the end zone. On second-and-goal, they tried a bootleg pass, but I wasn't going to let it happen. I grabbed that quarterback, Homer Jordan, by his shoulder pads and slung him around like a rag doll. That boy must still be spinning today. NFL teams noticed who I was that day.

GIL BRANDT was the Cowboys player personnel director

George Young [Giants GM] and I were at the Clemson game, and Taylor was unbelievable. He was lined up on the left side and they ran a play to the right. It was a fast running back. This guy looks like he's gonna go seventy yards for a touchdown. Taylor comes completely across the field and the guy gains about fifteen yards. You don't see many plays like that. George and I sat next to each other on the flight back to Newark, but we didn't even talk about it. Everybody had lockjaw.

TOM BOISTURE ran the Giant draft in 1981

I asked Bill Parcells to go down and take a look at him. He said, "What for? It's a waste of time."

"What do you mean?"

He said, "Well, the guy's a helluva player."

"Well, just go down and write a freaking report on the guy."

When he came back, I asked him, "What do you think?" and he said, "I don't think anything different than before I went down there. He's a top pick and one of the better linebackers I've ever seen."

Looking out for my future, I signed with two agents, Mike Trope and Ivery Black. Ivery had seen me kick ass in the Gator Bowl, and came knocking on my door before my senior year. "You got a chance to be the first player picked in the draft," he told me.

I said, "Get outta here!"

"The NCAA doesn't like this sort of thing," he said, "but there's no law preventing me from talking to you before you finish up here." Ivery explained that while he was an agent, he couldn't give me money at that point. His policy was to lend an athlete what he needed till he got drafted, when the money would be repaid.

What he wanted was to make sure I focused on my game and my skills, so he recommended I move off campus, away from distractions, and not even think about taking a summer job. He had it all worked out. If I agreed to take him on as my agent, there would be an initial payment of $500. I would live in the dorm until December, getting another $200 a month so I wouldn't have to work. After I moved off campus, my monthly payments would go up to around $350 to cover the added cost of the apartment.

All this sounded great to me, so I said to Ivery, "Do you

have the five hundred on you?" Ivery pulled out the cash and a contract, and I wasn't in a particular hurry to read it. "Let me sign that thing!"

Ivery set up shop at a Holiday Inn down the street from my apartment. From time to time he would come over to my place and cook dinner for me. My favorite was pork chops, black-eyed peas, rice, corn bread, and cabbage. And he was the one who turned me on to golf. We went out that first time and I was hacking up the first hole, but on the second hole, after I had rolled my drive two hundred yards, Ivery suggested that I try a two-iron. I nailed that sucker, and damned if it didn't go in the hole. An eagle! I started jumping around and screaming, and I was hooked. Two years later, I was shooting in the seventies.

The start of my senior year, Hugh Green, a linebacker/defensive end at Pitt, was the biggest man on campus according to the scouts, but then I started kicking some serious ass.

I became a terror. Now guys are watching film of our defense and are scared to play me. Barry Switzer, the Oklahoma coach, called me Godzilla, and that was about right because I had a bunch of King Kongs playing with me. We called our defensive front the Magnificent Seven. At the time, some people said there were only two teams that had defenses better than ours—the Dallas Cowboys and the Pittsburgh Steelers.

AL GROH

By LT's senior year, I'd moved on to Texas Tech. At that time we were running the veer option. One of the offensive coaches was kinda like, "Ah, this North Carolina team, they're not used to playing out in our league." I said, "Fellas, you better watch out for this 98, you haven't seen a guy like him."

The game was in the balance. North Carolina was ahead 9–3, and we're gonna try to run an outside veer. We're driving into the closed end of the stadium. LT hits the quarterback, causes a fumble, and recovers the fumble.

After the game, they told me, "We should have listened to some of those comments."

By the time of the NFL draft, I was The Man in college ball. As it turned out, Ivery would have been right about me being the number one pick if Saints coach Bum Phillips hadn't been trying to find himself another Earl Campbell and drafted George Rogers out of South Carolina. The Giants picked me second even though some of their veterans had said before the draft that they didn't think the team needed me. They were probably pissed that some hotshot rookie who hadn't played a down in the NFL would be making more money than them. When word got out that they were bitching because the Giants were ready to pick me, Ivery and Trope fired off a telegram advising George Young not to bother drafting me. Harry Carson and a couple of other veterans had to call me up and assure me that every-

thing would be cool. Harry even took me to dinner at Beef-steak Charlie's and made me feel welcome.

When I got to New York, the Giants rushed me to a press conference so they could show off their big prize. While Ivery and George talked money, I met the press.

"We have to get the people of New York behind you," Ivery told me. So he wrote me a speech about the great Giant tradition—great players like Sam Huff and Andy Robustelli and Rosey Grier—and how I'd wanted to be a Giant all my life.

The press ate that shit up. Those city slickers also liked it when this country boy said, "I like to eat quarterbacks in the backfield."

CHAPTER THREE

Before I could really settle in New York, I got blindsided by something that ripped my heart out. My buddy Steve Streater got into an accident that really fucked him up. Steve was my roommate at UNC for three years. He was crazy as I was, and like a brother. He was a great athlete—he was the number one pick in baseball in the entire nation when he was in high school—and with his ability to pull women we had some great times. He was a kick-ass defensive back and had been signed as a free agent by the Redskins, so it looked like we were going to be rivals.

Anyway, one night I'd gone out drinking with another Giant rookie, Dave Young, and I got back in the middle of the night and the phone was ringing. Ivery Black was on the line.

"LT, I've got some bad news for you. Steve has broken his neck."

At first I didn't know what in hell he was talking about because I was drunk and sleepy, but then, when I put it all together, I freaked out. First thing in the morning, I was on a flight to North Carolina. Some people would've worried about just leaving training camp all of a sudden, and the likelihood of the Giants coming down on them. But you know what I thought? "Fuck football." I didn't give a shit.

There's not much in life that scares me, but I was terrified of walking into that hospital room and seeing Steve. I wanted to keep it together and promised myself I would. I walked in there and saw his parents, and then there was the doctor, who told me Steve was asking for me. Then I saw Steve, my friend, a guy my age who was about to start on his pro career. And then this fucking doctor whispered to me that Steve's paralyzed. I lost it.

STEVE STREATER

"This is not you!" LT was yelling. "You've got to get up!"

He cursed the doctors and nurses out. He was telling them to get me up. He didn't care how. They calmed him down. He said he didn't want to play ball no more. LT was crying.

I had a weight tied onto the back of my neck with a halo on, so I couldn't move it. I couldn't move anything really. I was trying to wiggle my toes. I was trying to lift my leg. I was trying to do anything to make myself believe, which I still do now, and it's been twenty-two years.

I stayed in Steve's room all day, then fell asleep there overnight. I just could not believe it. Everything seemed meaningless. The last thing I wanted to do was go back and play football. But Steve told me to get on with my life, to play my ass off. And I told him that my first year with the Giants would be for him. Shit, *every* game would be for him. Steve is a fighter, and today he remains paralyzed from the waist down in a wheelchair, but he's never given up.

LEONARD MARSHALL,
Giants defensive end

What happened to his friend Steve Streater definitely had an impact on his life and definitely made him realize what God had given to him. And once he got that point, he knew he had to take it to a higher level.

When I got back to training camp, at first it was hard to get my head into it. But Bill Parcells, the Giants defensive coordinator under Ray Perkins at the time, knew how to keep my attention. Bill and I were close from day one. Of course, he was on my ass from the first day of practice. I had never had anybody ride me like that in college. Some guys need a coach badgering them every minute to get them motivated. I never needed that. You start all that yelling crap with me, and I'll tell you where to go. I would tell Bill where to go more than a few times. A love-hate relationship, I guess.

I wasn't awed by my new teammates. The Giants weren't exactly coming off a stellar season, and it wasn't like people were comparing their defense to the Steelers' Steel Curtain or anything. Hell, they'd gone 4–12 the year before. They could use some help. I'd heard of a few guys—Harry Carson and Brad Van Pelt—but once I got on the field with these guys, I knew they were no better than I was.

On the first day of minicamp, I was fourth team, behind John Skorupan, Mike Whittington, and Kevin Turner. By the second day I was second team. I thought I was doing pretty good, but on every damn play, Bill would not let up. Here I was, trying my hardest, and Bill was making me feel like I couldn't do anything right.

BILL PARCELLS

You try to find out what your players are gonna respond to. You might even do something that stings him. You're just trying to see what type of competitor he is.

MIKE DENNIS, Giants cornerback

I stopped in to LT's room on this particular day and found Lawrence was almost crying like a baby. He was laying across the bed pouting, stomping his feet on the ground, hitting the headboard. That practice he was dropping off into pass coverage, picking up backs, faking the blitz. He knew he could get the guy [quarterback] before he threw the ball. But Parcells was breaking him. He would say, "You look like a Doberman pinscher with your ears all pricked up ready to rush. Everybody in the world knows you're ready to rush."

Parcells would turn his engine up. He wouldn't give him a break. He used to say one thing over and over again: "Son, you're just like a ball in high grass. Do you know what that is?" Of course LT would say no. Bill would say, "Lost."

One day I'd had enough and finally said to Bill, "Listen, you either cut me, trade me, or put Skorupan back in . . . but you better get the fuck off my back!" Bill just looked at me and didn't say anything. A little while later, he went over to some of the older players and said: "I like that LT. Motherfucker's got a mean streak." I sure as hell did. The vets found out in a hurry that I meant business when we started running our conditioning tests.

BEASLEY REECE, Giants defensive back

He chose to run with the defensive backs and wide receivers . . . and matched us stride for stride!

In my first scrimmage, against a poor journeyman quarterback named Cliff Olander, I had four sacks and recovered a fumble.

HARRY CARSON, Giants linebacker

I was impressed right away by his quickness, and his closing speed. If somebody ran a sweep away from his side, he was able to catch them from the other side quickly, just pursuing.

Billy Taylor, a veteran running back who would become a good friend, lost his starting job because he couldn't handle me on blitz pickup drills in practice. He got screamed at every daggone day. Of course, as the year went on, Perkins—and everyone else—began to realize that *no* running back was going to keep ol' LT from the quarterback.

BUTCH WOOLFOLK, Giants running back

Whereas Harry Carson would run over you, LT would run over you or around you and leave you flat-footed. He'd embarrass you more than anything else. He had an array of rushes. He made me look stupid all the time. But if you blocked him one time, the next time you can expect the bull rush. He was gonna hurt you.

I remember standing on the sidelines for our preseason finale, against the Steelers. When Mean Joe Greene came running out with his gold shoes, I thought, "Man, I'm in the big time now!" These guys were legends, they'd been terrors in the league for years, and I was wondering if I was good enough to compete with them. I didn't wonder for long. I played two quarters and sacked their Hall of Fame quarterback, Terry Bradshaw, four times.

During a defensive team meeting, maybe the Friday before my first regular-season game, Bill said, "Okay guys, I want Harry Carson, Brad Van Pelt, Brian Kelley, Beasley Reece . . . and LT to stay." After all the others left, Bill looked at me and said, "I know you're wondering why you're here."

And I said, "Yeah." And Bill said, "Because everybody in this room is in awe of your talent. Because you can do things that a lot of people can't do."

Hearing him say that in front of the vets really propelled me. I said to myself, "I ain't gonna let that sonuvabitch down, I'm not going to let them players down." And every time I went on that football field, I wanted the guy across from me to be in awe of me, too.

No one had seen anything quite like me. I remember a big picture of me in the *Daily News* with the headline HE SHOULD BE OUTLAWED. I liked that.

DAN DIERDORF,
ex–Cardinals guard and TV analyst

We're getting ready to play the Giants LT's rookie year. I'm watching film with the other linemen, and our line coach. And we're just amazed at this number 56 flying from sideline to sideline. He had awesome speed. But none of us bothered to look at the roster, to see how big he was.

So we're on the field in New Jersey, and we're warming up in our end zone, and all of a sudden number 56 trots out of the tunnel. As he went by us, we all stopped and looked at him and said, "Are you shitting me? We couldn't believe how big he was."

People always ask me what made me so special. I think my first step was one of my best assets—I was very quick off the ball. It didn't hurt that I was fast for a six-three, 243-pound linebacker. There's raw speed and there's football speed. I was fast on a football field. I also knew how to run inside stunts—low to the ground. It's not just about making the tackle, it's about pushing that pocket protecting the quarterback. When you hit that pocket, hit it full speed, low, so when the offensive lineman hits you, you've got so much energy and power that you push him back, and push the quarterback out of the pocket.

I was never a big weight lifter, but I played a lot stronger than I was.

KARL NELSON, Giants offensive tackle

He'd come in the weight room once or twice during the off season and you'd never see him again, but I think if he would have taken care of himself he wouldn't have been as good a player. The thing that made him a great player was his total disregard for his body. Whatever he had in him he left out on the field. Some of the things he did on the field a sane person wouldn't do.

PHIL McCONKEY,
Giants receiver/punt returner

I never saw him do a push-up, sit-up, or toe touch.

Beyond my physical tools, I had a tremendous feel for the game, and I knew how important the simple things were. You can rush the quarterback and he'll be standing there so wide open that you can just tear his back up, but what would I try to do first? I'd go after the ball. I'd tackle with one hand, and swat at the ball with the other. Of course I wanted to make tackles. Of course I wanted sacks. But defensive players get paid to give the offense the ball. I played ball in the NFL like it was a sandlot game—get rid of the motherfucker in front of you, and go to the ball. Wherever that ball was, that's where I wanted to be.

I loved sweeps, too. That season, many teams made the mistake of running the sweep away from me. When offenses did it back then, they didn't leave anybody on the back side to block, so I ran across the field and would usually tackle the runner for little or no gain. Man, the thrill of chasing that sucker down from behind while the whole offense was so preoccupied with blocking what was in front of them. Havoc, baby, havoc.

While I was kicking ass in the preseason, something amazing happened back in Chapel Hill, where Linda was living with her mom. My son Lawrence Taylor Jr.—TJ—was born. I flew down there and held that beautiful child in my arms and I couldn't have been more proud. Man, I had a real job and now I was a daddy again. (Footnote: Yes, "again." In 1980, the beautiful Whitney Taylor Davis was born; she was being raised by her mom, my ex-girlfriend, Kathy Davis.) Some people might actually mistake me for a grown-up!

LINDA

He was happy. He was scared like most men are when they have a little child. He was scared to hold him.

Linda and I hadn't married yet because all I kept hearing was I'd be a fool to play in the NFL and be married. We were engaged—I'd proposed to her back in January while Ivery was in the car with us on the way home from the airport.

LINDA

Ivery said, "Don't you have something to give her?"

Lawrence pulled out this ring and said, "Oh here." He didn't say, "Will you marry me?" or anything like that. Just, "Oh here."

Okay, so I had no idea how to tell this special lady that I loved her and wanted to marry her. Still, I was happy she accepted and that I had landed a total class act. We got married the next year, on June 19. It was the smartest decision of my life. (Though maybe not hers!)

LEE ROUSON, Giants running back

LT was the most nervous player I've ever seen before a game, and I didn't understand it at first. He was always like that, shaking like a leaf. He was scared he wasn't going to be the best football player on the field that day.

My first regular-season game was our opener at Giants Stadium. We'd lost eleven straight to the Eagles, and I wasn't going to let that continue. Their quarterback, Ron Jaworski, was my very first sack victim. I wasn't even supposed to be rushing on the play. Harold Carmichael, their big-ass receiver, was out in the slot, and I was supposed to be out there to hit him. So I went out there, but he went in motion and then came back, and I got caught out of position. I was just a rookie, remember. I used to get confused all the time when the offense changed the strength of their formation and shit like that. My rule was: If you get confused, rush and get the quarterback on his back as soon as you can. So that's what I did. The back picked me up late and I had my first sack.

Jaworski had his head on a swivel for the rest of the game, looking to see where I was lined up. One time I yelled at him, "I'm coming to get you!" And I got him, all right. Bill was amazed that I was able to push through their offensive lineman, Stan Walter, and sack Jaworski. The guy was six-six, 290, something like that, which in those days was huge.

We lost that game, but I think the Eagles sensed that the tide was going to turn, that there was a new badass sheriff in town and he wasn't taking any prisoners. I also think it set the tone for future games against Jaworski. He'd spend the rest of his days looking over his shoulder to see if 56 was on his ass. And I usually was.

LARRY McCARREN, Packers center

Bob Schnelker, our offensive coordinator, gets up in a meeting and says, like Burgess Meredith in *Rocky,* "Guys, we're playing the Giants this week and they got this guy Lawrence Taylor, he's just a rookie. Guys, let me tell ya: I've seen Butkus, I've seen Nitschke, I've seen 'em all. He's better than all of 'em."

Early that year, we were playing the Cardinals, and I was supposed to drop into coverage. I had a better idea—I decided to sack Neil Lomax, and force a fumble. And I did. And then I did the same daggone thing a little while later. This time, when I came back to the sideline, Bill told me it wasn't in the playbook.

"Well, coach," I said, "we better put it in on Monday, 'cause it's a dandy!"

I realized early on that you don't have to make a hundred tackles to be The Man. Anybody can make plays when the game is out of hand. You have to make plays in critical situations. That's what it's all about. There are only six or seven times in any game that are critical situations, times where if you make a play, it can turn the tide. The key is to recognize when that is. It's not always first down, it's not always third down.

STACY ROBINSON, Giants wide receiver

I would watch him in the fourth quarter of a tight game. It's almost like his eyes would turn a different color. You know the whites of his eyes? They started getting this dim color.

Late in my rookie year, we played the Rams in a very tight game. There was a play where I blitzed and threw my left arm over Wendell Tyler and then grabbed Pat Haden around the neck for a sack. On the next possession, Haden fooled me with a play-action fake, but I recovered fast enough to make the interception and preserved the 10–7 win, and, as unlikely as it seemed, our playoff hopes. After the game, Perkins said that if I could stay healthy, "I think he'll go down as one of the best to ever play the game."

Anyway, I didn't like losing, and as I said, my goal was to help turn this team around. We started off 2–3 but finally got our shit together, had some fun, and kicked some ass.

LEON BRIGHT,
Giants running back/kick returner

Before we went out and beat the Cowboys to make the play-offs in 1981, LT stood by the door of the locker room and said, "Everybody reach in this box and take a can of Kick-ass. We're gonna go out there and kick their ass." I was like, "Damn! Let me reach in and get a can!" We're going out the door, reaching in the box, taking a can of Kickass.

We went to the wild-card playoffs against those daggone Eagles.

JOHNNY PERKINS, Giants wide receiver

Ray Perkins had it so you could not hit the receivers, so we had red jerseys on. We were practicing for the wild-card game and I reminded LT, "I got this red jersey on, you can't hit me!" Naturally, he hit me. He didn't hit me to hurt me. He was just letting me know he *will* hit. He said, "All right, Perk, get back over there."

We beat the defending Super Bowl champs 27–21. That was a sweet victory.

BILL BELICHICK, then Giants defensive aide

One of LT's single most amazing games was the playoff game in '81 against Philadelphia because he not only dominated on defense, but also dominated on special teams, forcing two fumbles by Wally Henry. He probably had better games on defense (some games against New Orleans and San Francisco come to mind), but not overall.

Thanks, Bill, but we ended up losing to San Francisco, 38–24. Part of the reason they beat the shit out of our defense? The 49ers were the first team to use a lineman to block me. They had John Ayers, a six-five, 265-pound guard, pulling all day like he was Joe Montana's personal body-guard.

So they were onto me. Man, I was angry about losing. I'd become so accustomed to winning I fully expected to go all the way to the Super Bowl. But overall I felt pretty good about my rookie season—I was voted both Rookie of the Year and Defensive Player of the Year, and I went to the Pro Bowl—and I knew with a few adjustments it would take a whole lot more than some lineman to stop me.

CHAPTER **FOUR**

I only started to realize exactly how much I was feared around the NFL after my rookie season ended. That's when players from other teams started telling me what went on during a week's preparation to play the Giants, how I was the focal point of their offensive meetings.

In my second year, I could look into these guys' eyes and see that these sonuvabitches were scared of me. It was a pretty good feeling, and it got even better when I began to know what I was doing. Brawn *and* brains, homeboy.

O. J. ANDERSON, Cardinals running back

Our wide receivers coach, Emmitt Thomas, called me, Roy Green, and Stump Mitchell together and said, "Do you guys want to see a real convict? A true convict can run the penitentiary. Come over here, I want to show you guys something."

It was a clip of LT jumping over Wilbert Montgomery

and sacking Jaworski. "Ain't no running back can block this man," Thomas told us. "We want our quarterback healthy for the whole season. No disrespect to you. This man is not human."

Damn right. I was the warden of that hundred-yard penitentiary. A teammate of mine once said that quarterbacks would take one look at me across the line of scrimmage and forget the snap count.

DICK LYNCH, Giants radio announcer

After one game, some of the Cardinal coaches rode the elevator down to the locker room with me. "He knocked the hell out of us," one of them said. "We'll be lucky to field eleven guys next week!"

The players went on strike in 1982, and we finished the shortened season at 4–5. Even though I repeated as Defensive Player of the Year and went to the Pro Bowl again, there's not a lot I want to remember about that season . . . except for maybe the game against Detroit on Thanksgiving Day. I had two plays that really stick in my brain. In one, I overpowered the guard and grabbed Gary Danielson with one hand and just slung him down like a bag of laundry. Then I just walked away, no big celebration. It was like, hey, this is what I can do and that's all there is to it.

Later came a more memorable play. I had done my

homework, and read the offensive set correctly, and I said to myself, "Wait a minute, I saw them run the same damn play two weeks ago!" When I saw Danielson drop back, looking to his left, I said to myself, "That sonuvabitch. I *know* he's not going to throw over here." So I drifted and drifted, and then I saw him spin around, just as he had two weeks before, and throw all the way across the field to the running back, Horace King. I was all over that shit. My biggest problem was making sure I caught the ball. They said I was a blur racing down the sidelines. I was so excited when I got to the end zone that I slid and skinned up my knees. It was a ninety-seven-yard interception return. We beat the Lions, 13–6.

JOHN MADDEN,
ABC *Monday Night Football* announcer

LT was the most dominating defensive player I think who's ever played. If he got to the point where he wanted to win the game, he didn't want to be blocked, and he said, "I gotta take this game over and change it," he could do it. And I don't know that there's ever been anyone before or after who could do that.

I hadn't even started that game. I was on the bench for the first quarter with a bad knee, and the coaches didn't want to play me too much. I didn't like that, and was acting like a baby: "Screw you, Bill! Don't try to send me in there. If you're not going to let me start, then I don't want to play." I was really pissed. But when Bill said, "LT, get in there," I'm like, "Where's my helmet?! Where's my helmet?!" I was ready to go out there without my fuckin' gear.

BYRON HUNT, Giants linebacker

He did not practice one play that entire week. Not one play. You know those old knee braces that had metal on both sides? They are the most obnoxious things you could ever wear and that's what he wore.

I'd had two really strong seasons now, and I wanted some more security, so I held out for a while during training camp in 1983. I wanted an extension and some more guaranteed money. I'd get restless just sitting around, so once I actually went out to Pleasantville and tried watching camp from a hill.

KARL NELSON

LT held out for more money in '83. He was standing on top of the hill watching practice one day. Harry Carson saw him and got down on his hands and knees and started snorting the white lines on the practice field. LT just laughed it off.

I had started messing with cocaine in my second season. It's not like I needed the coke—I was wired enough, believe me—but it was just something that was available, like beer, liquor, and, oh, here's a line of coke. It didn't affect my game, and I still felt that I was getting better every Sunday. Some of my teammates, like Harry the comedian, knew I was doing it, but I don't think the front office or coaches had any clue. Yet.

Anyway, I held out for almost three weeks, but I got nothing to show for it except that I missed some hot, sweaty practices. All the Giants would agree to was they'd think about it after the season was over. When I returned, I wished I hadn't. It was a frustrating year.

Perkins left at the end of the '82 season to take his dream job and coach Alabama, his alma mater. Then Bill Parcells became head coach. Some of the players didn't respond to Bill as well as I did. When a new head coach comes in, he's happy to have his chance, so he doesn't do everything necessary to make a team win—Bill was loyal to the guys who had helped him get the job, so he wasn't making big changes. We needed something to happen, though, especially on offense.

It got so bad, though, that Bill had to talk me out of quitting after we could only tie the dog-ass Cardinals 20–20 midway through the season. And when Harry went down with a knee injury, Bill moved me to his inside linebacker position. I hated it because I could no longer see the action coming to me. I couldn't take advantage of my field of vision, which is my God-given ability—to see lots of things happening at once. Instead there was this mess of centers, guards, tackles, all the big motherfuckers, running backs and the kitchen sink coming right at me. After games, I felt like I'd played ten years in the league.

I didn't do postgame interviews that year because I don't like to air dirty laundry, and our hamper was full. There were a lot of guys who weren't giving 100 percent. Some guys had become accustomed to losing. My rookie year the Giants were 9–7. In '83, we went 3–12–1. It was a shock. When we would lose a game, I would take it hard, man. I'd sit in my locker with my face in my hands. I remember Harry Carson telling me, "Hey, don't dwell on it. There'll be a lot of these."

I started showing up late for practice. And once I didn't show up at all. That day I got a call at home from Bill. He wanted to know where I was and I told him I was sleeping.

"You're supposed to be at practice," he said.

"I don't want to waste my time with a bunch of losers," I told him. He wasn't too happy about that. But out of respect for Bill, I went down and we talked in a car in a parking lot outside Giants Stadium. He needed me to show up and play. I understood that and I got back with the program. Of course, I still thought there were serious problems with the team, and they were on the other side of the ball.

There was a lot of resentment. We were the number one defense in the NFC, but what good was holding a team to ten points if you can't score but nine? Our quarterback, Scott Brunner, took a lot of abuse. He had played so well when Bill chose him over Phil Simms, but he played like a dog in '83. Our goal as a defense was to keep our offense off the field as much as possible. We figured that was our best chance to win. There wasn't any name-calling, just sarcasm and lack of respect. We'd see the offensive players walking to their meetings and we'd yell, "They need *more* meetings!"

RON ERHARDT, Giants offensive coordinator

Even as I called from upstairs in the press box, I could hear LT on the sidelines through Bill's headset when things weren't going well. He'd rant and rave at them and get 'em going: "We gotta get crazy out there! You can't play like that. We're really flat—come on, we know what this game means." He was worth his weight in gold. He wouldn't mince any words. Bill might say, "LT, get 'em in there [at halftime] and talk to some of those young ones and get our guys ready to go."

BUTCH WOOLFOLK

He'd watch the game and inspect it like he was a coach. He could tell you who wasn't doing their job. The coaches allowed him to rant and rave. He just went crazy in the locker room at halftime: "You bleeping guys are so soft out there; this is embarrassing; I can't believe you bleeping guys are not performing," spitting and screaming and cursing.

Even though we stunk it up that year, I believed in Bill. I just knew he was somehow going to make it happen for the Giants. But we needed better quarterback play and better players on offense. I was dedicated to Bill after that season—I liked his personality, and he was always fair with me. We were like cut out of the same mold—we didn't take a lot of shit and we desperately wanted to win.

KEN O'BRIEN, Jets quarterback

During a scrimmage against the Giants, I fooled LT with a pass to the tight end.

Parcells gets all over LT for getting beat. About ten minutes later, Pat Ryan came in for me, and called the same play. I remember thinking, "Don't do it, Pat." But he did, and at the last second LT sped up and picked the ball off—he had baited Pat into throwing it—and ran over to the Giants sideline and dropped the ball at Parcells's feet.

Bill almost didn't get a second season. One of the reasons he kept his job was because of me. This is a complicated story, but here goes. At the end of that '83 season, I'm sitting in my living room, and I get a call from Donald Trump. He owned the New Jersey Generals of the USFL, and he had signed Herschel Walker, the Heisman-winning running back out of Georgia. And now Mr. Donald Trump wanted to talk to me.

So I go down to his office—actually, it was his office *building,* the Trump Tower—and he gives me this *big* show. He takes me into this big-ass room, like a theater, and shows me a fourteen-minute video, "The Donald Trump Story." It was impressive as hell. Then he takes me into this big-ass office overlooking Manhattan, and he tells me that he wants me to help build the USFL, that he wants me to play for him. I said, "Well, I still have three years and an option left on my Giant contract."

He said, "I don't care. I want to do a futures contract with you." He said he'd pay me over $4 million over five years, and I'm like, "Wow!" because I was making like $190,000 a year with the Giants. Trump said, "You think I'm bullshitting? I'm willing to give you a million dollars right now to sign."

When he mentioned that million dollars, I didn't hear nothing else. I signed.

My agent was in town to talk with the Giants about restructuring my contract, but I didn't tell him about my deal with Trump. We have breakfast at some place in Hackensack, and he knows I'm antsy, because I keep getting up to use the pay phone. Finally, I come back and tell him, "I'm taking you shopping today."

Ivery found that hard to believe. He said, "Tight as you are, there's something up if you're taking me shopping." So we get in my car, and I drive around for a while. Finally, I stop at a BMW dealership and tell Ivery, "I'm going to get me one of these today." Then I told him, "I signed a deal with Donald Trump and he gave me one million cash. The money's been deposited in my account."

I expected him to be happy. He wasn't. "You're already under contract," he said.

"Yeah, but I signed a *futures* contract."

He wasn't pissed, but he was a little shocked. "Why didn't you call me a week ago and let me play the Giants against Trump?"

When I told him that I had to sign *that* day or give up the million-dollar signing bonus, he said, "You got screwed. That money's going to be outdated. Let me make some calls. There's a way we can beat this."

"I got one million in cash, man. I don't want to beat this!"

Well, I was wrong. Ivery and Trope met with Trump and convinced him that he had made a bad deal. They asked Trump if he'd release me from that contract if they could get him back his money plus a substantial bonus. Trump told them he doubted they could do it but said he was interested.

Ivery and Trope then met with George Young, and gave him the good news/bad news thing. They told him about Trump, but said they could cancel the deal—if the Giants were willing to buy Trump out. Which they were.

And that's how my contract wound up being reworked. Trump got his $1 million back and $750,000 over five years from the Giants. I got to keep Trump's $1 million and now the Giants were paying me—over the next six years— $650,000, $750,000, $850,000, $900,000, $1 million, and $1.1 million. Not too shabby.

DONALD TRUMP

This was a pretty good deal. I ended up selling him back to the Giants. I did it not because of the money; I did it because I never thought Lawrence Taylor should be in the USFL. I had too much respect for him as a football player. He was the Best. He was the Greatest, and he's also a wonderful guy. I really never thought his future should be clouded.

There was consternation throughout the NFL. They couldn't believe it. I told him, "You know what, Lawrence? At some point I have a feeling this league is just a shot in the dark. I have a feeling that what's going to happen is they [the Giants] are going to be coming back. You know I'd never stand in your way." So I let Lawrence go back to the NFL.

LIONEL MANUEL, Giants wide receiver

I looked at my first NFL check and wow! Nine thousand dollars! I'm flipping. I guess Lawrence must have heard me. He was in the seat in front of me on the airplane. He looks over his shoulder, I saw him open his envelope, and he says, "Here, homeboy, this is where you want to end up." I looked at his damn check after taxes. It was $58,000! I was upset then! "Wait a minute. Nobody makes that kind of money."

Then when the team arrived at the hotel, Lawrence had a limo waiting for him outside. He would pay somebody to take his luggage up to his room and he was gone. When we were going into the hotel, he was leaving. That was my introduction to football.

With the additional security, Linda and I grew our family a little more. Our second daughter, the adorable Paula, was born on October 6, 1986. I don't reckon I celebrated her birth in the usual way.

LINDA

He was away at a game. I don't know if he came back in town and went out somewhere and got drunk, or got drunk on the plane, but he showed up at the hospital drunk. He ended up throwing up in the room. Instead of the nurses taking care of me, they were taking care of him!

So now I had my contract and my family was getting more settled, but I was about to lose my coach. Young had met with Howard Schnellenberger, who had just won the college championship at Miami. The papers were already saying that Bill was out and Schnellenberger was in. Before I signed my new contract with the Giants, though, I had Ivery tell the Giants that I wouldn't sign unless they kept Bill. And, surprise, surprise, all of a sudden they love Bill. Schnellenberger stayed in Miami. Bill and I had a strong bond from that point on.

After the 1983 season, Bill started doing some heavy-duty gardening. He weeded out the troublemakers. He weeded out the guys who would sit around the locker room and bitch and moan all the time. He weeded out the underachievers. He weeded out the guys who just played when they wanted to play. He kept the fighters.

Bill didn't become a real head coach until he started making that place like a bus station. He was doing what had to be done, but I didn't like it at the time. My rookie year, it was fun going to work; it wasn't like a job. All of a sudden it was like a business. You never knew who was going to be lining up next to you. Guys would be in camp one day and gone the next. You didn't even get a chance to say good-bye. There was a lot of tension in our training camp before the '84 season.

I just wanted to win, and I wanted to take my play up another level, and Bill responded well to me. Yeah, I got special treatment. If I didn't feel like running at the end of practice, guess what? I didn't run. Bill wasn't too worried about what I did Monday through Saturday because he knew what I could do on Sundays. A lot of people look pretty good on the driving range, but what can they do once they have to play eighteen holes?

Some players didn't like the fact that I was given preferential treatment. But you can't bitch too much about somebody who's out there kicking ass every game. I used to tell 'em, "Listen, when you can do what I do on the field, maybe you can get out of running in practice, too."

Of course, there were times when I took things a bit too far and the coaches tried to rein me in.

JOHN WASHINGTON, Giants defensive end

LT skipped a morning practice in training camp and Parcells chewed him out in front of the team and announced that LT was being fined $10,000. LT said, "Okay, fine, that's what, thirty thousand dollars now?"

As far as I was concerned, that was money well spent.

RICKY BARDEN

He did something I had never heard of. The Giants coaches wanted him to do some weight lifting, and said they would fine him $500 every time he missed a session. He was supposed to work out twice a week, so he just sat down and wrote 'em a check for $16,000.

I didn't work out during the off season. My philosophy was, when the season was over, I was off. And I mean *off*. I wasn't going to run none, I wasn't going to lift none. I wasn't going to do anything. The way I got in shape was to take as many snaps as possible in training camp. I'd be dead tired and stay out there.

LIONEL MANUEL

Once he told Johnny Parker, "You know what, Johnny? I was here before you, and I'm gonna be here when you leave. Stop fucking with me."

JOHNNY PARKER, Giants strength and conditioning coach

I think he got into this Superman persona; Superman didn't lift weights. And I know he had a weight room in his house. Still, I think Lawrence almost felt it would be a betrayal of his image. He was a guy who could play through any pain. He might not have done everything the way you'd

want him to to prepare for Sunday, but on Sunday he would kill himself to win.

Now don't get me wrong. I wasn't sipping margaritas while the team was practicing. I was busting my ass out there, too. It's just when it came to inconsequential and boring stuff, I just couldn't get into it.

KARL NELSON

At my first training camp, I remember everybody was busting their ass, but then we see this guy walk onto the field and he doesn't have his shoes tied and his chin strap's not buckled. I'm thinking, "What's the deal with this guy?" But I soon learned that if LT's got his shoes tied, you better watch the hell out, and if he's got his shoes tied *and* his chin strap buckled, you're dead.

Clearly I was doing something right. I'd been in the league three years, and in the Pro Bowl three years. Backs and tight ends couldn't block me. Working with Bill and Lamar Leachman, our defensive line coach, I developed a technique against a guard where I'd smash into him, stop him cold, then knock his hands away so he couldn't get a hold of me and slip inside him if he was trying to push me to the outside.

Double teams were a pain in the ass, but not always. The two guys—say a tight end and a guard—sometimes didn't block with the same intensity, so if I was able to slip the more physical by using a double slap with an uppercut, I'd just run over the other slacking sonuvadog and give a hurting. I developed a whole range of maneuvers, adding a more technical side to the wild abandon I usually brought to the field.

JOE JACOBY, Redskins offensive tackle

Our offense and formations were geared toward where he was gonna be. He would always line up away from the tight end the first couple of years. That's where all the motion and different things would start with the tight end, or H-back, motioning back toward where he was to try to get two people on him. Somebody was always chipping and helping out to give him something else to think about. Even receivers would come down and chip on him just to keep his head on a swivel to slow him down a second or two. They countered by moving him around. It was a chess game.

PAUL ZIMMERMAN,
football writer, *Sports Illustrated*

The single best play I ever saw him make was he put a rush on against the Redskins, Joe Jacoby was in his way, he threw him. I can't remember the name of the guy, but somebody else went to pick him up, it might have been [guard] Russ Grimm; he threw him, too. Theismann scrambled out of the pocket, flushed by Taylor. Taylor ran him down fifteen yards downfield. He had thrown six hundred

pounds' worth of linemen, and run down a 4.5 quarter-back. That's the greatest defensive play I've ever seen in football.

I also started taking more of a leadership role that year. In training camp, I ripped into Bill for telling the press that Harry Carson, who was a holdout, should look up the meaning of *leadership.* I said, "Maybe management should look up the word *honesty.*"

I started fast in '84; I had eight sacks in the first four games. But before long I found myself going through the motions. I got bored. I got over that, though. Always did. Bill always found ways to get me over that hump.

WELLINGTON MARA,
Hall of Fame owner of the Giants

He was the ultimate put-it-all-out-in-the-field guy, and he made everybody around him play better. That was the only way he knew how to do it.

There were a few times when I thought I was sleepwalking, though. I got my bell rung just like everybody else who plays this violent game. I had a few concussions, and the Giants coaches had to hide my helmet whenever that happened so I wouldn't sneak back onto the field. Ronnie Barnes, the trainer, would give my helmet to the equipment man, who would lock it in a trunk somewhere. A couple of times I grabbed a teammate's helmet and went back in the game. After the coaches caught me doing that, they ordered my teammates to not give me *their* helmet.

PETE SHAW, Giants defensive back

If there was a good play or a bad play, he'd always tell Belichick, "Run that back." If somebody got knocked out, he'd say, "Run that back. Whoa, whoa, whoa. Slow it down." Everybody would say "Oh shit!" He just loved the way people played hard. If you got hit, so be it.

We were playing the Washington Redskins once, and I got kneed square in the head by their big, bad, rugged back, John Riggins. Knocked the shit out of me. I stood up, but I didn't know where the hell I was. I'm in the middle of the field and Harry Carson yells at me, "LT, get lined up!" But I'm still thinking, "Where the fuck am I?" Harry had to call a time-out and get me to the sidelines. It was maybe an hour later before I realized what had happened.

Riggins was probably just giving me a little payback. The best hit I ever had came against Riggins my rookie year. This was the second game of the season. Riggins was a beast, a real load, especially on the goal line. He hasn't said shit to me all game, because I'm a rookie. Anyway, Riggins came over the pile at the goal line, and I caught that sonuvabitch head-on. BAM! He went straight down. When he got up, he just said: "Good hit, rookie."

I could take the heat, as long as the hits were clean. It drove me out of my mind when guys would try to cut me.

Eric Dickerson tried to in a game against the Rams, the opening game of '83.

ERIC DICKERSON, Hall of Fame running back

It was my first pro game and we had a play where I had to block Lawrence Taylor. The running backs coach [Bruce Snyder] said, "Just cut him and the ball will be out [of the quarterback's hand]." Okay, we call a play, he rushes, the ball gets out, I cut him. He grabbed me by the arm, looked me right in my face, and said, "Hey, don't fuckin' cut me."

I kept waiting for LT to laugh, or crack a joke. But he just stared at me. No laugh. When I went back to the sidelines, I told the running backs coach, "That man said, 'Don't cut me!' Fuck that shit. I'm not cutting that man again! That's Lawrence Taylor." I just had a lot of respect for him.

Sometimes, though, I couldn't control what would happen once I made contact. One of my low moments came when I broke Joe Theismann's right leg on *Monday Night Football* in '85. I've never seen the tape of it, so I don't know how the hell he got into that situation. I remember that I rushed him, and Joe saw me late. I was just about to put the hurt on him when he stepped up in the pocket, trying to get away. I grabbed him, and started turning him, trying to bring him down like he was a bull. Unfortunately, he fell in an awkward way, and then I heard a SNAP, and then guys on both teams fell on top of him. He was screaming, "You motherfuckers broke my leg!" There's nothing worse than to be hurt and out of breath and tired, with a whole bunch of people on top of you. I've been in that situation, and it feels like you're going to suffocate. I don't care if it's only three seconds, it's the longest three seconds in the world. So I just start pulling people off the pile.

The doctors and trainers sprinted onto the field, and . . . well, let Joe tell the rest of it.

JOE THEISMANN, Redskins quarterback

I remember everything. It was one of the most hard-hitting games I'd ever participated in. The intensity level was incredible. As I went back into the pocket I felt pressure from the left side. I felt somebody grabbing my shoulder. I heard *pow pow*, like two muzzled gunshots. It was my leg breaking. The pain was beyond description. I remember [Redskins trainer] Bubba Tyer coming up on my left side, asking, "You all right?" "No!" I never went into shock. I said, "Please call my mom and dad and let them know I'm okay." Joe Gibbs kneeled down on my right side and said, "Joe, for six years we've been together. Joe, you've meant so much to this football team. Joe, this is a heck of a mess you've left me in." We both chuckled.

They put me on a stretcher and were wheeling me out; I had to stop the gurney. Harry Carson had talked about retiring. I yelled, "Harry, don't you go retiring. I'm coming back." He said, "That may be the case, pal, but it ain't gonna be tonight."

The next day the nurse comes walking into my hospital room and says, "Mr. Theismann, Mr. Taylor's on the phone. Would you like to talk to him?" I said, "Give me the phone."

"Lawrence, is that you?"

He says, "How you doin'?"

"Not very well."

"Why?"

"You broke both bones in my leg."

"Joe, you gotta understand, I don't do things halfway."

We both laughed.

I've never seen the injury. Lawrence used to do a television show and I was on it a couple of times. Neither one of us would look at it.

That night changed my life. I was the most arrogant, egotistical SOB on the face of the earth. It forced me to take a long, hard look into who Joe Theismann was. I don't look at what happened as a tragedy, but as a blessing. It might have had a profound effect on his life also. I asked him one day on his show and he said, "What I learned was that no matter how great you are in this game, it can be over in an instant." I get the sense he rededicated himself to football.

I didn't feel guilty—I didn't try to hurt him. I was just doing my job. I had a lot of respect for Theismann. I think he was one of the few quarterbacks I played against who could have played in any era. Very smart. Joe Montana was another one—he could hurt you so many ways. And I'd have to put the guy from Denver in there, John Elway. And Dan Marino.

And Jaworski. Brett Favre and Terry Bradshaw are also on that list. And so is Phil Simms.

Phil got off to a bad start with the Giants; if he could have played the first part of his career like he played the latter part, he would have set all kinds of records. But early on, he was more of an I—I—I guy instead of a team guy. His attitude then was, "I'm doing great, you guys are fuckin' up." He wanted to get his three hundred yards passing in a game, but he didn't want to get 'em with twenty or thirty short passes. No ball control for him. He'd be happy with six long passes for three hundred yards, even if he's six-for-thirty. He became a *player* when he started hitting the tight ends and the backs, eating up the yardage—controlling the ball, and the game.

Phil and I ended up being good friends, but we sure didn't start out that way. I didn't like him at first. I can't remember what year this was, but it came out in the papers that blacks weren't allowed in some of the prestigious country clubs in the area. When I found out that Phil was a member of a club that didn't have black members, I was real upset. He tried to tell me, "No, no, no, blacks have played there and so and so."

I said, "Bullshit." Every time I would look at him, all I could see was a bigot, and I didn't think we could win as a team if we had white guys on this side, black guys on that side. But that's how it was on the Giants up until about '85. Since Phil had said that blacks were welcome at his club, I called his bluff. I said, "Okay, let's go play."

He took me out to his club one Tuesday, and the people

there looked at me like I had just landed from Mars. And I tried to be the biggest ass I could be. I wore my hat backward, didn't tuck in my shirt . . . and I was real loud out on the course, yelling shit like, "In your face!" when I'd make a putt. But Phil took it all in stride, had fun with it, and he ended up rescinding his membership at that club and joining one that didn't discriminate. That was the beginning of our bond. And as time went on, and as he became a truly great player, I looked for his respect as much as he looked for my respect.

I also think Phil's personality changed that season. He started having fun with us. He started to loosen up, be a more sociable guy who—every now and then—would even come out and hang with us. My first few years, it was like a front-office guy had entered the locker room when Phil Simms came in. He set himself apart from the rest of us. We were the blue-collar workers. But when he put on the hard hat, and when he started taking responsibility for his mistakes, started getting more people involved in the offense, started worrying less about his stats and more about winning, he became a better quarterback and a better person. He became a leader. Sonuvabitch would come back to the sidelines sometimes and say, "Goddammit, I fucked that up." He became one helluva quarterback.

ERIC DORSEY, Giants defensive end

During camp, Bill Belichick made all the defensive players—rookies and veterans—stand and introduce themselves and say what college they had attended. LT was the last one to go. He sat way in the back. I think Belichick had to say something to him, because he wasn't going to get up. When he finally did, he said, "I'm LT. Don't fuck with me." And sat down.

CHAPTER FIVE

KIM

To his family, he's Lonnie. Very few people know Lonnie. A lot of people know Lawrence. Everybody thinks they know LT. I don't know LT. I used to see LT on the field on Sundays. LT was the worst thing that ever happened to him. He became Superman, so New York allowed him to do a hundred in a fifty-mile-per-hour zone. He could bust up things as long as he performed on Sunday.

The fans in New York really loved me, but the fans at North Carolina had loved me, too. The biggest adjustment for me in the pros was that there were so many more fans, so many more people asking for your autograph. They'd come at you on the street, in the bathroom, in a restaurant while I was trying to eat. I'd try to accommodate everybody, sign everybody's autograph. Then I'd take a bite of my food and it would be cold. I don't count how many cold meals I ate—it's a wonder I didn't starve to death. The novelty of *that* wore off very quickly. Fans are great, but they want what they want, and they want it now.

KEVIN HELLER, pal, jeweler

On the final Saturday of the 1981 season, after the Giants had beaten the Cowboys 13–10, we had the end-of-the-year party at the Underground. One fan after the next came over to shake his hand. "Special K," he said, "the next guy who comes over to shake my hand I'm gonna punch in the mouth."

"Listen," I said, "do you understand you're the biggest thing to hit New York since Mickey Mantle? If you can't accept adulation, go fucking home. These people pay your salary."

LT wasn't in the mood to hear it. "Fuck you, Special K."

I didn't see LT again until the Jet game the next day in the Shea press box. Lawrence came over and apologized. He said, "You're right, you're right." I said, "I know I'm right."

When a lady I didn't know later threw the "I pay your salary" thing in my face, though, I reacted a little differently.

DYLAN PRITCHETT

We were enjoying ourselves over some drinks and music at the local Hilton when a persistent woman kept pressing

Lawrence for an autograph. She said that her father had Giant season tickets. She bought Lawrence a drink, and he returned the favor. After several polite refusals by Lawrence, she returned and snapped, "You have to sign this. My father pays your salary." Well, Lawrence reached into his pocket, took out a hundred-dollar bill, and said, "Here's the portion of the season tickets your father pays my salary with."

You can save a thousand lives and never be called a life-saver. I was truly grateful for my fans, as long as they didn't come between me and my food or me and a good time. Then there were the fans with an agenda—Redskins fans were behind one of my worst games ever. We were in D.C., and I went out for some drinking the night before. We were out *well* past our curfew, but these Redskins fans were feeding us free drinks all night. We're talking shit; they're talking shit, right? And I'm just getting blitzed. I was drinking beer, I was drinking Scotch . . . I was just having a good old time, right?

The next day, I remember getting up and feeling like I was completely dehydrated. On the field, it was hot as hell, so I was dying. But every time I motioned to Bill, "Hey, get me outta here," he would motion back, "Keep your ass in there." And, my luck, it was one of those games where the defense stayed on the field forever. I had never been that tired. I went to the locker room early, before halftime, because I was so dehydrated. After the game, I was gone, toast. The trainer had to hook me up to I don't know how many IVs.

Of course, that wasn't the only time I played a game with

not enough sleep. Many times I'd be out all night, and then have to take a lot of that over-the-counter speed truck drivers take to stay up.

BUTCH WOOLFOLK

He never seemed to need much sleep. After a long night, he'd come into the locker room, take a shower before the team meeting and drink all the Scope he could, and sit in the back of the room. He drank so much liquor it would come out of his pores. You could smell it.

I never played when I was high. I had some of my better games after I had been out late. I'm not saying it was a good thing to do, but I made it work for me. I put more pressure on myself in those situations, because I'd be thinking, "Damn, these guys are counting on me, and I fuckin' stayed out all night." A couple of times I rolled in at around eight in the morning on a game day. I did that once before we played the Cowboys . . . and had three sacks.

DONNELL THOMPSON,
UNC and Colts defensive tackle

When the Giants came to town for a preseason night game, I showed Lawrence around town before the game. At about twelve o'clock [noon] we hit all the bars. I had a hamstring pull, but Lawrence didn't know it. Lawrence didn't know I wasn't playing. We were out from twelve o'clock to four-thirty, five o'clock. Lawrence said, "Man, we're gonna catch hell tonight." I said, "Yeah, man, it's gonna be rough." So we had to leave about five o'clock and get to the stadium and get dressed. I'm in my street clothes. Taylor's looking for me on the sidelines. He calls me out just before the game: "What's up? You're not playing?" I said, "Oh, I forgot to tell you, I got a hamstring pull." He was pissed.

I got him wasted, and this fucking guy goes out in the first quarter and gets three sacks! That is the Lawrence Taylor story. You just can't hold him down.

Byron Hunt was my roommate on the road in the early days. Anybody who stepped into our hotel room back then knocked over beer bottles strewn all over the floor. My favorite cities for partying were Phoenix (wild women over there), L.A, Washington (well, before they took all the strip joints off 14th Street), Atlanta, and . . . Hell, how many cities have NFL franchises? The best party city of all, of course, is New York.

BYRON HUNT

Early on, we shared a house, and we had some memorable parties in that place. One night, I remember that there was either a guy or girl in every room and every closet in the house, either sleeping or having sex. And that was a three-bedroom house. A study, living room, kitchen, dining room, pantry, basement . . . Oh, I forgot the shower—there were two or three people in there, too.

We were just living the dream in those days. We would have a maid come in once a week, which wasn't enough. We had two things in that refrigerator: Budweiser and what was called a Strawberry Shake—a strawberry-flavored penicillin for any disease you might get from being with the wrong women.

I loved the big city, the bright, bright lights and all the action. The clubs and the bars were open all night and I took full advantage of those bad boys. By '83, on a typical night I'd pick up one of my pals and start our adventure at a bar in Teaneck and then take Manhattan by storm, bouncing from Studio 54 to the Underground to Sweetwaters to the Cellar to Rascal's to Bentley's to the Hasbrouck Heights Sheraton and the Front Row, wherever the party was. But first, after partying in Teaneck, there was a stop to be made.

I'd go get some coke from some Spanish guys up in Harlem on 133rd Street. You'd walk into the apartment to buy coke and there'd be one guy with a .38 who would be standing there with the gun in his hand. There'd be another guy sitting at a table with the scale. You'd tell him how much you wanted, he'd measure and put it in a bag. I'd buy about six, seven hundred dollars' worth, then leave, and look out world.

CHRIS SILEO, former general manager of the China Club

I never saw LT get sloppy drunk or coked out where he was fucked-up and everybody knows he's all fucked-up. LT

never got like that. I thought with him, one of his problems was he could control it so well, because he was the kind of guy who could get really fucked-up and still function.

Maybe it was my beverage of choice.

CHRIS SILEO

Chivas and milk. They still say it's the most disgusting drink they ever made.

To keep myself entertained, I'd do stupid shit, like stand on a bar stool, then dive off into a handstand. Or pull out one of my old college tricks and chew some glass. Drinking pitchers of kamikazes can do that to you.

Sometimes we'd party with guys on other teams. Some of 'em were my friends—I had friends on every team, and I had a lot of friends in the NBA. One time some guys on the Houston Oilers tried to mess my game up by sending two girls to my hotel the night before our game against them in Houston, one for me, one for my roommate. Snuck them in after curfew.

BYRON HUNT

We ordered a case of champagne from room service. Lawrence tells me two girls are going to be coming over after bed check. We had a four o'clock game the next day, so we figured we had plenty of time. There's a knock on the door, and two gorgeous girls walk in. Lawrence and I look at each other and just smile.

We pour the champagne, and have a light conversation, "Where are you from? Blah-blah-blah." That went on for a couple of bottles of champagne, then they go into the bathroom. We're thinking, "There's something good getting ready to happen now."

When they open the bathroom door they got nothing but towels on. Things were looking up. We continue to drink champagne, talking some small talk. By the sixth bottle of champagne, the towels are gone and Lawrence is in one bed and I'm in the other bed and we are having a good old time. Every once in a while we'd look over at each other and we'd both be thinking, "Isn't pro football great?"

We thought *that* was the good part. Then the dark-skinned girl goes in the bathroom and the light-skinned girl says to us, "I'm going to make her crawl up the wall." We're not sure what that means, but we're interested. The dark girl comes out and the light-skinned girl starts touching her and kissing her, and they go at it for a long time. And we're just sitting there, holding our peckers and a bottle of champagne. By this time I'm guessing it's four o'clock in the morning.

I don't remember what time we finally passed out. All I know is we caught the late bus to play the Oilers and the girls were still in the room, knocked out.

The great thing about this story: We beat holy hell out of Houston.

Those Oilers had themselves a solid game plan. Too bad it didn't work. I had a great Saturday night, and an even better Sunday afternoon.

There were no hard feelings—hell, I would do it, too. If you're playing a team, and they have a player that's pretty hot, especially a running back or wide receiver or someone like that, you might call up an escort service and just send a couple of hookers to the room, because you know daggone well there ain't too many guys gonna turn 'em down. You just try to get them to stay up as long as they can. It was like a joke. Then you talk about it after the game: "Did you enjoy yourself last night?"

Being out late a lot meant I had to develop a system for beating the team curfew. I made it known that I wanted to be the first one for bed check. And I was dressed to kill whenever one of the coaches knocked on my door. It got to the point where they stopped even checking my room. They didn't even want to *know* if I was there or not.

The only coach I had to worry about was our defensive guru, Bill Belichick. He'd always been a ballbuster. Bill Bedcheck. He was as smart as they come when it came to football; always had a way to combat anything and everything an offense could throw at us, but he didn't have what they call "people skills." A lot of coaches, if you were late or something, would let you slide. If Belichick caught you, he was going to bust you. He was like the kid who was always going to tell in school. If it was his night to do the bed checks, I'd be there. The only other time you had a chance of catching me in my room was if we were playing someplace where it was real cold. Real, *real* cold.

JOHN CIMILUCA, Giants ballboy

He used to pay me twenty, sometimes fifty dollars to lay in his bed at bed check. Coach [Pat] Hodgson and [fellow aide] Ralph Hawkins used to do bed check. Once or twice a week LT would find me up in the dorms or in the field-house doing laundry, and he'd go, "Meet me up at my room at ten-thirty, ten-forty-five."

The very first time, he said, "You gotta do me a favor. Lay in my bed and keep all the lights out. When they come knocking on my door, you'll be laying in my bed. Give a lit-tle grunt."

The coach would open the door with his key, and since the lights were out, as long as there was a body in LT's bed and a grunt, all was clear. I'd stay in bed for fifteen minutes until the coaches went to bed and the coast was clear.

If you got caught missing a meeting, or missing curfew, Bill would say: "If you're late for bed check, it's five hundred dollars. If you do it a second time, it's a thousand. If you do it a third time, it's two thousand. And if you find some pussy out there worth two thousand dollars, come wake my ass up, 'cause I want to go, too."

Some training camps, the coaches were lucky if I stayed in my room one night a week. Sometimes I'd go home. Or out.

I remember one time, a teammate left an inflatable sex doll in his bed before sneaking out. We didn't get back in until about five o'clock in the morning.

CASEY MERRILL, Giants defensive end

One night in training camp LT and I were creeping out the back door after curfew and we heard this noise that made us jump back. We figured it was a coach. It was Harry Carson sneaking back in.

We went to this bar just to have a beer. It was crowded and some guy purposely leans forward and pops me in the chest-shoulder area. Behind me was LT. The guy then does the same thing to LT. Not a smart decision. This guy was probably five-eleven, 180 pounds, but in a split second, LT has him in the air, over his head, like in a military press. Then it gets quiet as he tosses the guy so that he lands on top of a table and you hear a crash and breaking glass, sorta like in a Western movie. I'm just thinking about the physics of it: How did he get the leverage to get that guy up over his head and then get him to fly that far across the room without making a big effort?

We walked out of the bar at that point and got into his car and went to another bar. I didn't say anything to him about it and he didn't say anything to me.

How was I going to enrich my life and meet new and interesting people if I didn't go out? For example, I met the young Mike Tyson at the China Club. Mike wasn't as big then as he is now. We became friends. He was a street guy who was given a whole lot all at once, and it overwhelmed him. When he was in prison for that rape thing, he called me one time and said, in that high little voice of his, "LT, they got me locked up in here!" And I said, "Yeah. Mike, I know. It's been in every paper. You've only been there two years!"

I seem to attract controversial people. Maybe because I'm that type of person, too. But I stick with my friends. A lot of people tell me that it's bad for my image to be friends with O. J. Simpson, but I don't look at it that way. I got my opinion of what went on that night and ain't nobody going to tell me who I can associate with. If he's my friend, I don't look at what he's done, as long as he doesn't do nothing to me.

As for myself, I know my limits, and I have my standards. For instance, I'd never do a threesome—two guys and a girl—but I'd have taken two girls anytime. Hell, one night I came back to the team hotel with *five* women. Whoever was checking curfew that night turned a blind eye. He told me later that he would have told Bill if I had played like shit the next day. But I didn't. Me and those five women had a little prayer meeting. Just kidding. Hey, what's *any* guy going to do with five women? What *can* you do? It's not that I want to screw five women at the same time. Or could. The excitement is can I get all five of them into the room at the same time butt naked? The rest of it's just a picture show. Just like watching porn on TV, and I was working the remote control.

BYRON HUNT

Studio 54 DJ Frankie Crocker used to have a party for the Giants and Jets. If you had a wife, you didn't take your wife. If you had a girlfriend, you didn't take your girlfriend. It was one of those wild, wild parties where you'd have sex with a lot of different girls in one night.

When my teammates and I would go out, I would pay for everybody's drinks—I'm always the Money Man. I can remember some $3,000 and $4,000 tabs.

LIONEL MANUEL

The wildest thing about strip bars and athletes, since we do have more money than the regular customers, if I put down one [dollar], maybe Ottis Anderson puts down two, someone else puts down five; that's the competition thing. All of a sudden, the bartender comes out and lays out a bunch of tens or twenties, sometimes fifties, just lines the whole stage [around the dancers] up. At first it was like, "Who in the hell is this?" After a few times you knew. It was LT. That was his introduction.

Sometimes, LT would take over the bartending duties, and he'd pour drinks on their [dancers' and waitresses'] breasts, like a wet T-shirt contest. Whatever wild thing came to mind, Lawrence would do it without hesitation, because he could get away with it.

LT wouldn't stop there, of course. Sometimes he would

remove his shirt and slide down the pole just the way the dancers would do it. He might even pull his drawers down; you just never knew. We'd get our money back out and act like we were gonna give *him* some money.

Talented, aren't I? I should point out here that not all of my teammates partook of the high life. Some guys did, some guys didn't. Anyway, game day, we had to be on the field at 12:05. I would usually get to the locker room about 11:40. One time in St. Louis I was a little late getting to the stadium and my teammates had to stall—doing extra stretching in the locker room and shit like that—so I could join them on the field for warm-ups.

LIONEL MANUEL

We went on the field for pregame warm-ups, and the coaches were asking, "Anybody seen Lawrence?" No one's seen Lawrence. So trainer Ronnie Barnes had one of his men head back to LT's hotel room. The guy's out on the floor. I guess his brother came up the night before, and they had a tequila party. As we were coming back in from warm-ups, they were bringing him in. This guy is out. They were putting ice towels on him, giving him coffee. They dressed him, they put his uniform on, taped his ankles. The sonuvabitch had four sacks.

In Cincinnati in '85 some reporters—on their way to breakfast, I assume—found me sleeping in the elevator, standing up, riding up and down. I don't remember that elevator, but I know I had one of the worst games of my career that day.

BYRON HUNT

Once Lawrence checked in a hotel, he was like Osama bin Laden—you couldn't find him. He switched cars with a friend who didn't play for the Giants so he wouldn't be followed.

On road trips, players get off the bus and pick up their room keys downstairs in the hotel lobby. That might take fifteen minutes, but once, by the time I got upstairs, Lawrence was already entertaining guests.

I also liked to gamble. I just loved Atlantic City. In fact, I had about $110,000 worth of $500 chips in a safe-deposit box in a shaving kit in Clifton, New Jersey, under my manager's name and Paul Davis's name. On my way to AC, we'd pick up the chips and then go do some damage. The most I ever lost probably was $150,000, but I've won as much as $200,000. In case a game ever popped up, I'd carry $5,000 or $10,000 in my pocket and keep another $100,000 in a brown bag in the car. Unlocked, of course.

Carrying all this money around, there was always the potential for some asshole to steal from me. Once, in Puerto Rico, I'd won about $30,000. I didn't want to bring any carry-ons onto the plane, so I put it into my luggage. They run it through a screener first, then you take it up and check it in. I realized I had the money in the luggage, so I ask the security guy if I can take something out of my bag. He said no, and he and his buddies watched me check that bag in. By the time I landed in Miami, even the change in the bottom of the bag was gone.

GARY JETER, Giants defensive end

We were on our way to a mall in South Jersey. Nobody could sit in the back of his car. There were beer cans and bottles all over the floor. I opened up the glove compartment and a four-thousand-dollar Rolex watch he had gotten for an autograph signing four or five months earlier fell out, along with a bunch of papers. I started looking and saw all these "New York Giants" envelopes were open. They were checks. I gathered about ten checks totaling seventy-five, eighty thousand dollars, that weren't even cashed. They still had the stub attached. I said, "Man, what are you doing? You got all this money here you haven't cashed." He said, "Hey, I haven't lost it. I just haven't gotten around to going to the bank."

PHIL McCONKEY, Giants receiver

One time he burst into the locker room before a game with a gleam in his eye and announced, "All right, fellas, let's see what I can do on eight hours of sleep!"

Yep, they all cracked up at that one. Granted, there weren't too many times I had eight hours of sleep, or anywhere close. What can I say? I had a hard time with Just Say No. I couldn't go anywhere without someone offering me this or offering me that. That's why I did most of my sleeping during meetings. I used to lie down on the floor in the front of the room, the farthest spot from the coaches. Steve DeOssie and I would turn our chairs over so the backs became like recliners. If I needed a nap, DeOssie would watch over me, and if he needed one, I would watch over him. And I had to really watch that sonuvabitch because he had a tendency to snore.

STEVE DeOSSIE, Giants linebacker

I remember one film review session when Belichick was in one of his usual, grumpy moods. This was after a win, but whenever the tight end would beat you deep or the guard or tackle would run over you, Belichick would make it seem like you had just been whipped by the worst player to ever play the game. He'd say, "AAAANNNYYYBODY but this fuckin' guy . . ."

So finally, Lawrence has enough of this crap. He jumps up, flips on all the lights, and says to Belichick, "Look, you little motherfucker. You never hit anybody when you were at Wesleyan or wherever the fuck you went to school. I'd be surprised if you ever saw the goddamn field. I'm sick of this." And he storms out. Belichick didn't even blink. He just continued harassing everyone else.

After the meeting, I found Lawrence asleep on the couch in the players' lounge. I asked him what the hell he'd been thinking, yelling at Belichick like that. He smiled and said, "I'm so fucking tired. Belichick was keeping me awake with that crap. I had to get out of there!"

Another time I was snoring while Belichick was running film of the previous day's practice, which showed me just jogging through some drills. "Look, man," I said when I woke up, "you either get me on Thursday or you get me on Sunday." They were content with getting me on Sunday.

BILL BELICHICK

What really got him going and generated feedback was when we watched Tampa Bay's defense and we made sure to make a really big deal about [linebacker] Hugh Green. We'd really exaggerate it and say, "THAT'S the way we want to do it. Look at him take on that lead block!" After about two of those comments, Lawrence would start fighting back. He'd say, "If he's so good, why didn't you draft him?" We'd say, "Oh, we're not saying he's better, we're just admiring his play."

The most memorable defensive team meeting I ever remember happened in Dallas. I had met this tall, light-skinned black girl and I slipped her into my hotel room early Saturday evening. So she and I are having some fun, and she says she wants to put handcuffs on me. Fine. I'm up for anything, right? Except when we're done, she can't find the keys. And I have to go to the team meeting at nine o'clock that night.

CARL BANKS, Giants linebacker

The meeting starts, and we're looking for Lawrence. Belichick gives his spiel; but still nobody's seen Lawrence. Last time anybody had seen him, he was in the hotel, but that's all we could say. Fifteen minutes later, we hear that he's outside the meeting room. But he won't come in. For some reason, he's got hotel security going to his room.

Even though I had the handcuffs on, I came down for the meeting. I'm sitting outside the room, and who sits down beside me? Father Moore, the team priest, and a great Giant fan. He starts talking to me and I'm saying to myself, "Oh, man, I know I'm going to catch hell for this."

CARL BANKS

He finally comes into the meeting room, and he has on a huge white sweater, but his arms are underneath it. The lights are off, and as he walks in, we all hear *clink-clink, clink-clink.* He sits down and I say, "What the fuck you got on? What kind of bracelets you wearing?"

He says, in a whisper, "Shut the fuck up." Then he leans over and says, "Bitch handcuffs me and takes the key!"

Needless to say, everybody that's sitting up in front with us hears this and busts up laughing. It works its way through the room, and gets to Belichick. Now, Belichick was a hard-ass, but he likes a good joke, too, so he says, "Uh, Lawrence, why don't you come up to the chalkboard and diagram this next play . . ."

By this time, somebody sticks their head in the door and says, "Lawrence, they're waiting on you outside." Security had found a key, I guess. So he gets up, goes outside, takes the handcuffs off, and then comes back in like nothing's happened. By then we were all in hysterics.

If you're counting up my vices, you've already got drinkin', partyin', gamblin', and sexin' (if that's not a word, it is now!). But the most devastating vice of all was the druggin'.

CHAPTER SIX

I had heard about cocaine in college, of course, but it was considered taboo, so I didn't touch it. I used to put away some beer, though. I didn't graduate to liquor until I started worrying about my weight in the NFL. When you're young, you can drink a twelve-pack of beer and run it off the next day. But when I got to the pros, why get sloppy with beer when I could just have a mixed drink?

My heaviest drinking was in college. We used to call the University of North Carolina the beer-drinking capital of the world. On Saturday nights, five of us would get a keg, drink that and maybe two bottles of Jack Daniel's, and then go out on the town. And, like I said earlier, we raised fuckin' hell, man. I smoked marijuana every so often, but I didn't like it.

The first time I used coke was midway through my rookie season. I was sharing a house in Passaic with Byron Hunt and Dave Young. We were throwing a party and some dude said, "Try this." So I did. What I remember is instant euphoria.

LINDA

His rookie year I found this white powdery stuff in his pocket. He said it was cocaine but that it wasn't his. He said he was holding it for one of his roommates. I believed him. He was so against drugs back then, not once did I think the cocaine was his.

After that, I would use cocaine if I was at a party and somebody was passing it around, but I wasn't going to buy any of that shit, no, it was just a social thing for me. In '84 it became addictive, but I didn't see it that way. In my entire life, I never let anyone or anything control me. I would tell friends, "Taylor controls the drug. The drug don't control Taylor." But I saw the addiction for what it was in 1985. That's when all hell broke loose. That's when I smoked cocaine for the first time, and it was like, "Oh shit, I have to lie down." Then I said, "Damn. I need some more of this shit." Before long, I learned how to freebase as well as Emeril knows how to cook.

LINDA

When he first started cocaine, he was just snorting it, but then he started taking a filter out of a cigarette, mixing the cocaine with the filter, putting it back in the cigarette, and smoking it. That's when I started noticing the plastic bottles in his car, and the baking soda.

BOBBY CUPO, my former manager

LT never sniffed [cocaine]. He always used to roll it up in a Salem cigarette, and he had a whole procedure. He'd first empty out half the tobacco from the cigarette. Then he'd grab the filter with his teeth and pull the damn thing out, rip it in half, and put the filter back in. He'd put the line out there and he'd suck the cocaine up into the cigarette using the cigarette like a straw. After that, he'd take the tobacco, put it back in the cigarette still open at the top where you light it. Then he'd twist the end.

I went from using about half a gram every two to four weeks to an eighth or more in one night. I used to buy a gram, then all of a sudden I was buying an eight ball—that's three grams. Then I stopped buying eight balls and I'd buy a couple of ounces a week. Go through an ounce in a day or two. It got to the point where there would be times when I'd be standing in the huddle and instead of thinking about what defense we were playing, I would be thinking about smoking cocaine after the game.

I don't even want to know—much less tell you—how many times Paul Davis and Linda combed the mean streets in the middle of the night trying to drag me out of the bars and crack dens.

LINDA

At times he would go missing for days on end. I'd have to call around to try to find him. He'd come home, and we'd argue and fuss. My only weapon with him was, "I'm going to tell your mother." That would scare the shit out of him and he would always straighten up . . . for a few days.

BOBBY CUPO

Linda would call me up at two in the morning and tell me Lawrence was walking barefooted in the middle of winter in the woods looking for people that he thought were looking in his window.

It became my job to help LT beat his growing paranoia. For a week, he moved in with me and I drove him to practice and picked him up. When he was at practice, I'd rent movies to keep him settled down when he got home. If the guy likes a movie, he'll go see it ten times, twenty times. It lasted about a week. He said, "I got so much rest I'll end up killing somebody."

The Giants were playing at home, so I drove him to Giants Stadium. I said to him, "Okay, Taylor, you did great. Let's not screw up." He said, "No no, I'm just going out for a little while [after the game]. I'm just gonna hang out." *Bam!* I didn't see him for another week. I didn't hear from him, nothing.

Finding coke was easy. I don't know a city I've ever been in that I didn't know where I could get it. I even bought cocaine in Utah, in the middle of nowhere. Suppliers hung around the team. You'd see them around Giants Stadium, too.

After my urine turned up dirty before the '85 season, Bill tried to help me by sending me to someone in New York, but I didn't want any help. I didn't want Big Brother—the Giants or the NFL—watching me every second of every day. That's why I started carrying a little aspirin bottle and getting a clean teammate to piss for me to beat the random tests.

BUTCH WOOLFOLK

I didn't drink or smoke or do any drugs, so LT would say, "Meet me in the bathroom." I peed in the cup for him a couple of times.

I'd then put that bottle into my jock, get my test bottle, go off to a stall, pour the urine into their bottle, and give them clean urine. It's all in my first book.

Later, they had someone stand behind me while I faced the urinal. I beat that, too, with a soft squeeze bottle, a Visine bottle. When I stood at the urinal, it was just a matter of reaching down and squeezing the bottle instead of my dick.

But they'd have to find my ass first. Once a player tested positive, then the NFL was allowed to do random tests. It was Ronnie Barnes's job to get urine from me. He would tell me to meet him at a certain spot right after practice, and more often than not, I wouldn't show up. I bet he collected that urine maybe one out of ten times.

The cocaine cat first got out of the bag when I was visiting Ivery at his place in California. We were sitting at his rattan bar just talking when my nose started bleeding.

"What's wrong with you?" Ivery said.

"I got a cold."

"Bullshit. You've been doing cocaine!"

I went on to my next lie: "Somebody introduced it to me in New York. Don't worry, though. It's just recreational use." I don't think I fooled him, though. He knew, and he knew that people were starting to talk.

BILL PARCELLS

He wasn't the same guy. They never are.

GEORGE MARTIN

When we first heard about it, Parcells's first response was, "George, if we don't get this guy help, he's not gonna make it." We were on the inside; we had our suspicions long before the general public. Parcells genuinely cared more about LT the individual than LT the football player. We'd go off to the side, or we'd hang around after practice, and he would say, "George, if we really care about this guy, we gotta get him the help he needs."

I worked behind the scenes to map out a confidential

game plan for possible treatment. That was one of my responsibilities at that time, and I knew how to kind of marshal the resources. We didn't want it to become public knowledge. We wanted to assure Lawrence that his private life would not be dragged through the mud. I'd done extensive background checks on facilities to make sure it was a turnkey operation. When and if he needed it, it was ready to go.

LINDA

The worst night was when Paul Davis and I dragged him from a Hackensack crack house. I had gotten a call from someone that LT was in there. Nothing was going on in the apartment. There were no drugs or anything. I went to open up the bedroom door and I couldn't open it. He opened it, but when he realized it was me, he closed it again. It was him and another female in the room. I told the owner, "If you don't open the door, I'm kicking it in, so you better get him out of there." I kicked the door so hard I put a hole in it. Then I told the owner [a second time], "If you don't get him, I'm kicking this door in." Then Lawrence finally opened the door and came out, and I grabbed him and said, "You're going home now." Of course, he didn't want to go. He came home with me, and we argued and fussed. I tried pleading with him to get help. He proceeded to go downstairs, and when I went downstairs, he was taking a lamp apart. I didn't know if he was trying to electrocute himself. I just had to constantly watch him the whole time because I was afraid he was going to leave again. Finally, he went to sleep.

Thank the good Lord above for Linda. Without her I don't see how I could have survived. She kept working on me to go into rehab. What really convinced me I needed to get help was an incident at the Pro Bowl. A reporter confronted me with the rumors that I was doing crack. He said, "Nobody's writing this, but there are whispers that you might be doing something, because the Giants are having you followed." I knew then that I was in trouble, and in March of 1986, I made my little trip down to Houston.

GEORGE MARTIN

My preference was the Hazelton facility in Minneapolis. I was surprised when I learned that LT had checked himself into Houston Methodist Hospital, but I was happy. I didn't care if it had been on Mars.

Ivery took me to Houston Methodist, where I checked in under the name Paul Davis. Then he called my mom and told her what was happening.

IRIS

I couldn't take details. I couldn't talk anymore. I couldn't handle it. That just made me totally sick. My stomach was turning. I just cried.

I thought I was in a psychiatric ward, and it looked like a jail cell. No way I was staying there, so Ivery got me into a $1,500-a-day suite in a different hospital. Paul Davis again. I had a private room and would order food delivered from the outside, but I still wasn't happy about being in there. In fact, I was extremely agitated. In a therapy session, a middle-aged woman couldn't fit a hammer into an outline on a pegboard, so I grabbed it out of her hand and slammed it in myself, then walked out.

To the golf course, my detox tank.

I think I had been in Houston three days when Howard Cosell came on the radio and told the world that I was in rehab somewhere in Texas. The press came after me the way sportswriters used to pounce on the free buffet in the Giants press room. They didn't let up for months. The papers ran some of the worst stories I've ever seen. They just completely dogged me. "The Giants don't deserve this," and "He let the team down." Shit like that pissed me off. My answer was, "Just look at my stats!" Who the hell was I letting down? I was letting myself down if I was letting anybody down. I think the 12-Steppers call that "denial."

CLARENCE

After Lawrence went through his first drug rehabilitation, we told him he should come home to Williamsburg, but we never had no long heart-to-heart talk about his problems. It does no good to have long conversations with Lawrence. Until he decides, "This is the way I'm going," the more you push him, the more he backs off.

"I'm going to get myself straight," he said, and we believed him. I didn't think nothing could control him like cocaine did because he had such a strong will.

JOHN "J.D." MORNING, a D'Fella

I was the one who would confront Lawrence about the drugs. It was basically, "This is not what we do. We play cards, we sing, we talk about how we're gonna be great. End of story."

I was embarrassed by all the drug stories when training camp started in '86, but Bill made it easier for me to handle the media by limiting their access. I concentrated on football. And got piss-tested every week. Meanwhile I just tried to keep myself busy and played lots of golf while trying to avoid lectures from well-meaning people.

GEORGE MARTIN

When LT returned following rehab, he made it a habit to avoid me. I was going to come to him with advice which he did not want to hear. I didn't have a whole lot of stock in golf therapy. He insisted it was working for him. I wasn't a convert at that time.

I came back mad and focused that season. The team was on the verge. We'd gone 9–7 in 1984 and made it to the playoffs.

In 1985, we went 10–6 and lost in the playoffs to the Bears, whose defense would lead them to the Super Bowl championship. We were getting so fucking close and I kept on winning those awards and going to the Pro Bowl each and every year.

So in '86, rejuvenated again, I played with a vengeance. Belichick always liked to show people the play where I almost sacked Cardinals quarterback Neil Lomax just as he dumped the ball off in the flat and then tackled the back fifteen yards downfield. I rushed off the line, got cut, got up, rushed the quarterback, and just as I saw him about to throw the ball, I didn't even turn to see where he was throwing; I just turned around and ran. And exploded into the back from behind and jarred the ball loose and prevented the tying touchdown in the last two minutes.

RON JAWORSKI

In '86, running back Keith Byars was our number one pick. I'd been playing against LT for five years now, so I know that when you play the Giants, you think protection first, at all costs. I remember sitting in our offensive meeting when I suddenly realized that Keith Byars—a rookie—is going to have to block LT. I was not feeling very good about this. I remember going up to our coach, Buddy Ryan, after our offensive meeting and saying, "Don't you think you have to slide the line toward LT?"

Buddy, in that Kentucky drawl, says, "Keith Byars can block him. LT's just another human being. He puts his pants on the same way."

> LT had three sacks in the first half. He jumped over
> Keith Byars for one sack, did an arm-over for another sack,
> and knocked Keith right over into me for a third sack.

After the three sacks, Jaws was nervous and I remember him getting under the center and yelling, "Where's LT?" I popped up my head and said, "Don't worry, I'll whisper in your ear when I come by."

Casey Merrill told me the Eagles had a $1,000 bounty on me. Ron Jaworski says he doesn't remember anything like that. Here's what I remember: You got rewards—$300, $500, something like that—for a knockout. Knock somebody out of the game. You hit somebody on the kickoff team and they had to come bring a stretcher to get his ass out of there, you'd receive a little something in your envelope for it. There's a big difference between a big shot and a cheapshot. Cheapshots were never any good. I used to leave Monday's practice with a pretty hefty envelope.

The way I got into the starting lineup my first year playing high school ball was by hustling. I did my best damage when I chased, so I chased all the time. When I got into college and the pros, it felt like there were two speeds—my speed and everybody else's. One other thing: You can go chase, but you have to catch the guy! And the only way you're going to catch him is to take angles, which I had learned a long time ago. And always hustle. Run as hard as you can until they blow that whistle.

BILL ARD, Giants guard

I remember him running through two pair of shoes one game. His foot went *through* his shoe. The seam just exploded. He came over to the sidelines and said, "The next time it happens I'm gonna sue these motherbleepers!" Just think how powerful he must have been for his foot to go through his shoe.

One play that set me on my way to winning the league MVP that year came against the Redskins. They were running a sweep. I went upfield to force the run, the back cut in, he got away from the corner and was on his way down the sideline for the winning touchdown, but I was able to spin around, and chase him down from behind, and strip the ball. Stripping the ball is what they teach now. I can say, "Hey, I brought that to the NFL."

I almost broke Mark Gastineau's sack record that year, which was twenty-two at that time, and has since been broken by Giants defensive end Michael Strahan . . . with Brett Favre's help. I had 20.5 sacks going into the last three games, but the teams we played put everybody and their mama on my ass; they were not going to allow me to break the record against them. No matter where I lined up, I'd have a guard, tackle, or tight end on me, and then have the back stay in to chip me. We were getting eight sacks as a team, but I wasn't even getting close to the quarterback. I would have liked to have set that record.

We destroyed the 49ers in the divisional playoffs, 49–3,

which was real satisfying because they'd always kicked our asses and stood in the way. Next, we had to beat the Redskins a third time in the NFC championship game. With that type of rivalry, it's hard to beat a team two times in a season, much less three. But I didn't give a shit. I really wanted that ring. I remember an interview with John Dockery, a TV/radio reporter who wears the Super Bowl III Jets championship ring. "Hopefully, we'll get to the Super Bowl and get a ring like that," I told him. "The closer we get to the title, the better this team becomes. With the grace of God and Bill Parcells, who may be the same people, we may get there."

The key to the Redskins game was a little fat guy who wore number 5 on his back, Sean Landeta. Why? Because the wind was blowing strong as shit. Their first punt went seventeen yards. We had great field position that whole quarter. And when they did drive the ball, Sean would punt it way down there. Second quarter, now we have to play against the wind. And I remember Sean's first punt; he's punting down by our end zone, and the punt returner is standing on our twenty-five. Landeta kicked that sumbitch forty-seven yards into the wind! *Bam!* And the crowd went crazy. The sideline went crazy! His second punt was also forty-something yards. He made the wind a no-factor for us. He was the star of that game. We won 17–0. We were 14–2 that year. Well, 17–2 if you count the postseason.

I remember walking off the field after the NFC championship, and it was covered with confetti. Our crowd was throwing all kinds of shit, man, and you could barely see to the other sideline. The Super Bowl wasn't as exciting,

because you're always chasing to go to the Show and we'd been frustrated so many times before.

For Super Bowl XXI, I had a chaperon the whole week to make sure I didn't get in trouble. I didn't even party with teammates the night before the game. Everywhere I went, Ivery was there. Well, almost everywhere.

MARK COLLINS, Giants cornerback

I found myself across from LT's room during Super Bowl XXI in Pasadena. I'm going to my room, I go in and out, and I see him go in with a different girl each time. One was Spanish, one was white. I said, "Damn! That's a bad dude!"

WILLIAM ROBERTS, Giants offensive tackle

At Super Bowl XXI in Pasadena, Parcells warned the team that Big Brother would be watching. Bill said, "Six of you guys are going to be followed by NFL security." We all knew what that meant, so we said to ourselves, "Well, we know LT's going to be watched, so don't ride with him."

GEORGE MARTIN

During Super Bowl XXI week, Belichick's up there espousing the game plan and everybody's so attentive. He's going over a critical piece of defensive material which involved Lawrence. Lawrence was sitting in the front of the class at this point. He had his typical Lawrence hat on, shades over his eyes, and head down as if he were looking at the game plan. So Belichick says, "On this particular play, it's gonna be your responsibility. Okay, Lawrence?" Lawrence doesn't respond. "Lawrence, you got that?" Lawrence doesn't respond again. Belichick walks over to him and lifts the shades off his eyes. He was sound asleep. He didn't chew LT out, which wouldn't have worked anyway, but he used him as an example to get everyone else's attention. He said, "This is not to be tolerated; our mind has to be right."

Whatever, I was pumped to play. Some reporter asked me when I knew I'd be ready, and I told him, "When you feel like slapping your mama." We obviously weren't ready to slap anybody's mama in the first half. Everything was going their way. Shit was happening so fast that we couldn't settle down and get our minds straight. That's the worst feeling for a defensive player. Especially for me. San Francisco used to do it to a defense, and Denver did it to us. *Boom,* they come out with a reverse, then a twenty-yard pass, then a little flea-flicker, then a double reverse . . . I was saying, "Whoa, whoa, whoa! Settle down."

We went into the locker room at halftime, and Bill doesn't say anything. He's pissed and guys are moping around. I felt it was my duty to say something, so I said, "Listen, guys: We didn't play no type of football. The score is ten to nine, and they got every break, and we played no Giant football what-soever, not one iota of Giant football. We're about to go out

here and kick these sonuvabitches dead in the ass." And we did. We played so well as a team, and Phil had his career game and we won 39–20.

When the Super Bowl was over, I showered, went to my hotel room, went to sleep for a few hours, then went down and had a little something to eat with my family. Everyone was so excited, but by then I felt deflated. It was like, "Okay, game's over, what's next?" I'd won every award, had my best season, finally won the Super Bowl. I was on top of the world, right? So what could be next? *Nothing.* The thrill is the chase to get to the top. Every week the excitement builds and builds and builds, and then when you're finally there, and the game is over . . .

And then, nothing. I felt that familiar itch. And it needed scratching.

CHAPTER SEVEN

PETER KING,
football writer, *Sports Illustrated*

I was at a dinner not long after the Giants had won Super Bowl XXI and LT was being honored as Pro Football Player of the Year. He kissed my wife Ann's hand very regally. This is a guy who 90 percent of the time never gave us [reporters] the time of day. We were vermin. We were gum on the bottom of his shoes. So he acted like such an incredibly perfect gentleman that the only thing I concluded at the end of the night is he must have been high.

Nineteen eighty-seven was a bad year in many ways. In August, I failed my first, official NFL random drug test, which gave me "one strike" in their program. Three strikes and I would be banned from football. Then there was a strike of another kind: the players walked out after the first

two weeks of the season. I wasn't really into it, though. I stayed out for a while, but I had no problem with *my* contract. I had already been through a strike in my second season, and all that did was cost me money. I wanted to play. What was I going to do? Sit around and smoke crack?

The NFL was using replacement players and continuing with the season, so after a couple of weeks, I decided to cross the picket line. I called Bill and told him, "I don't know if one man can win a game for you, but I'm going to try." Lord knows he needed my help—the team was 0–4.

BYRON HUNT

Lawrence had so much loyalty to Wellington Mara that he felt like, in my opinion, that he had to come back and play. Mara looked at Lawrence like a son. The Giants had protected Lawrence in a lot of ways as far as some of the off-field stuff that was going on.

The most memorable game was my first one back, against the Bills at Orchard Park. I was, as Bill put it, "a man against boys"; they did everything they could—legal and illegal—to stop me.

PETER KING

The game was such an ugly, sordid, terrible affair in which two players blocked Taylor on every play. Buffalo was called for holding him seven times. He was tag-team-wrestled the whole day. In the second quarter, the guy lined up across from him, a guy named Jim Schulte, a guard, kneed Taylor right in the face. It was just professional wrestling. So in the third quarter, when Taylor was sure nobody was watching when they were away from the play, he took his fist and drove it hard into Schulte's throat. He said, "How do you like THAT, sucker?" After the game, he goes up to Schulte on the field and Schulte balls up his fist, bracing for a fight. And Taylor goes, "Hey, you cheapshot bastard, good game." Taylor just loved it.

MARV LEVY,
former Buffalo Bills head coach

We had brought in Will Grant, a former Bills player who was out of shape, to play center. Lawrence blitzed over center on just about every snap, and Will got called for holding six times in the first half.

At halftime I said, "Will, you've been called six times for holding!"

He says, "Hey, that's good, because I was holding him every play!"

We lost 6–3 in overtime, but it was some of the most fun I'd had in a long time. I even got to play tight end! It was football the way it was meant to be played, sandlot-style. Before the games, the replacement players—most of whom had never been in an NFL game and, after the strike was settled, would never again be in an NFL game—were coming

up to me for autographs. After the game, it was, "Take a picture with me! Take a picture of me!" This was my teammates *and* opponents.

The players settled with the NFL a week later, but I kind of wish they'd never come back, that we'd never played that season. Why? That was the season I pulled my hamstring tackling Eagles quarterback Randall Cunningham, who was an amazing scrambler. That was the start of my downfall as far as injuries. All week Eagles coach Buddy Ryan had been telling the press that I wasn't quick enough to catch Randall anymore. I knew he was playing mind games, but I was like, "We'll see about that."

It was third-and-long, and he dropped back, rolled to his right, and then took off running, and I took off to catch him. I caught him about a yard short of a critical first down. But there went the hamstring.

JOHNNY PARKER

Lawrence was playing what we call the "spy" technique. He would be behind the line of scrimmage shadowing Randall Cunningham. He was over on his side of the ball; he didn't line up in the middle of the formation. And then Randall scrambled to his right, away from Lawrence, and it just happened to be right in my line of sight. I could see both of them perfectly. Randall Cunningham was a young man, and very fast. He took off, and then I saw Lawrence accelerate after him. And I can't explain it. It was as though you're watching a film with some of the frames cut out. Lawrence got from point A to point C without you even seeing Lawrence get to point B, and he dove and caught Randall by the shoe. It was the most phenomenal thing I've ever seen. He pulled his hamstring on the play. Of course he played the next week.

Yeah, but it never really healed properly and I'd feel its effects for the rest of the season.

ERIC DORSEY

LT was using electronic stimulation on his hamstring without success, but I had an alternative treatment that was becoming popular. You could crush up Advil or aspirin and mix that with DMSO and it healed even faster. So I invited LT over to my town house, where I'd been mixing aspirin with the DMSO. There was a pile of white powder under my kitchen table. I think when he first saw it, it was sitting there on a plate. He walks in, looks at it, and says, "Ahhhh . . . what is THAT?" with a big smile. I'm like, "OhmiGod!" He probably thought I had a little white gift for him.

We finished in last place with a 6–9 record. I was hoping things would get back to normal the next year, but the bottom fell out when I got busted by the NFL for a positive drug test again in August of 1988. Nobody bothered to call and tell me I was suspended for the first four games of the regular season. I found out while I was listening to the radio driv-

ing to the stadium for practice. I turned around and went home. I was devastated. I cried like a baby.

LINDA

The day Lawrence learned he had been suspended may have been the longest day of my life. I knew he was back on drugs, but I didn't know that he had been suspended. In the bedroom, Lawrence was broken, distraught. He kinda broke down crying, saying his life was over. He knew he had let a lot of people down. It was just a miserable day for him. He didn't talk much. I told him it would be okay, that everything would work out. He'll finally get the help he needs.

Lawrence barricaded himself in his room. Reporters came. George Martin stopped by and spent more time with Lawrence than anyone else. We were just kinda trapped in the house. I don't think he came out of the room at all.

I should have known better, but I had given in to the coke again. Now it was time to pay the price. It was a terrible price. I didn't know what to do. I felt my whole world was over. I don't know how I got through it. It was the most embarrassing thing that had ever happened to me. On the outside, everyone thought I had straightened my shit out, but I had this motherfucking secret that I didn't think anyone would discover. Hey, who was gonna outsmart LT? Well, now everyone knew. I was worried about my family, my friends and my fans. I had hurt the people who loved me.

GEORGE MARTIN

I was at home getting dressed for work to go to the stadium when Linda called me. She said, "I need you over here right away." She put Lawrence on the phone. He was sobbing. He was hysterical.

When I got over there, Linda was visibly shaken. Lawrence was in a fetal position in his bedroom, crying. I felt helpless. I stayed the entire morning, telling him the sun will rise tomorrow, telling him that this would break lesser men than him, telling him that his family was still intact, telling him his friends would rally around him, and I said a prayer for him.

I heard what George was saying, but I wasn't really listening to him.

There were camera crews camped outside my house, so in the middle of the night, Linda and I piled into the car and drove to Connecticut to stay with Beasley Reece and his wife, Paula, at their farmhouse. That's where Beasley, who was now working for a television station in Hartford, convinced me to tell the whole story. "They're going to chase you until the story breaks," he said. So I had Beasley make a live interview available to everyone. I told him, and everyone else: "Prior to 1985, I felt I was a casual user; in 1985, I became an addict."

What made this bust and suspension even more embarrassing was that I had come to training camp talking about how I was taking the game more seriously. I had even put in an $18,000 weight room, of all things, in my Houston home, because I wanted to improve my upper-body strength so that I'd be able to play the run better.

I guess the writing was on the wall when I got into a traffic altercation—past curfew, naturally—a couple of miles from our training camp. The kid said I cut him off; I told the Giants he was tailgating me and flashing his brights. He stopped in front of me and wouldn't move, so I got out of the car. He quickly locked his door, so I started yelling and ended up kicking his door a couple of times. He drove off scared to death. He went to the police station and filed a complaint.

The next day, a reporter showed up when I was coming out of the Giants' lunch hall, and handed me a copy of the police report. Which I promptly tore up and deposited in his shirt pocket. We ended up settling out of court. I paid $300, something like that.

The media wouldn't leave me alone. During the suspension, Barry Stanton of the *Journal News* in Westchester found me at a public golf course in New Jersey. "What the fuck are you doing here?" I said.

"I'm here to talk, if you want."

"Get the fuck away," I raged, and swung two golf clubs in his direction. I couldn't believe my eyes when Stanton started to leave. "Is that all you want?" I asked.

"I tried," he said. "Now I can tell my boss that I asked you to talk and you wouldn't."

I was confused. "Why would you come up here? Why is it anybody's business what I do?"

"You're a public figure."

"I should be allowed to do what I want to do. It's nobody's business."

Truth was, I was everybody's business, from day one.

When I came back to the team after my suspension, I read a prepared statement to the media: "Regrettably, I've made some mistakes in the past, some of which will invariably follow me for the rest of my life. There is nothing I can do to change that, so it will be very wise for me to concentrate all my energies toward my future."

Now I had two strikes against me. One more fuckup and I was gone, banned from football. Now that I was one strike away, when there were no more mulligans, I had no fear that I would mess it up, because football was more important than any drug that I could take. Everything I had accomplished in life to that point was through the game of football. I didn't want to lose it all.

HERB WELCH, Giants defensive back

He wasn't as happy. He was more jaded when he came back. It took something out of him. He just kinda climbed inside of himself for a little while. I just wanted to know was he okay? If there was anything I could do for him. I remember him being what I thought was sincere and pretty honest about the whole thing. He said this to me, it wasn't a problem 'cause it couldn't be a problem.

Wellington Mara is one of those rare owners who cares about you as a person, not only as a commodity. He said,

"You have to have hatred for the crime and compassion for the criminal." Mr. Mara made it loud and clear that I would have to be serious about my rehab program this time. I knew I'd be tested by the NFL at least twice a week from that point on, even in the off-season.

Dr. Joel Goldberg, who was director of career counseling for the Giants, guided me to Charlie Stucky and the Honesty House in Stirling, New Jersey, to undergo my NFL-mandated treatment. Goldberg advised outpatient treatment for me, knowing me well enough to understand that I just could not be locked up in some ward.

DR. JOEL GOLDBERG

Because he has such a thirst for life, it wouldn't have worked keeping him in a hospital. I thought Charlie would relate to him well. I had been on the board of directors at Honesty House. He had a lot of experience. He was a spiritual man, and I thought they would connect.

Charlie Stucky was an old Giant fan and a recovering alcoholic who also knew Wellington Mara. Charlie says that when he first met me—in 1985, three mornings a week as an outpatient—he was afraid that when we'd argue I would lose my temper, charge the huge desk he used to sit behind, and throw him out the window. Let's just say that I had plenty of anger in me.

One time we were sitting on the same side of that desk watching a film on alcoholics. I watched that film for about fifteen minutes, then stood up and screamed, "I am not an alcoholic, I never was an alcoholic, and I don't know why you got me doing these things!" I yelled this three times, but halfway through the third time I said to Charlie, "Ah, shit. I know I'm not going to convince you." I knew that Charlie knew I had a problem.

I used to hate making those Monday-morning drives from my house to see Charlie, because of the traffic. Charlie and I had been working on anger management when I stormed into his office one time practically shaking with road rage. "There's one thing we're not talking about this morning," I roared, "and that's anger, because I wanted to drive right through that fucking fence! One word about anger, and I'll pick you up and throw you through that window." Guess what: We didn't talk about anger management that session.

When we first met, he told me, "If you continue to use, they'll take the game you love away from you. You're not going to be in control."

That hit home and it motivated me throughout the rehab. I told Charlie, "We're not going to let that happen." And we didn't. I stayed clean for the rest of my days with the Giants.

In my first game back from the suspension, it was back to business. I sacked Mark Rypien on the third play of the game and forced a fumble and finished with two sacks in a 24–23 win over the Redskins at RFK Stadium. But my attitude wasn't right. Before a game in November against the Cowboys, I told Bill I wasn't into it. I wasn't sure if I wanted to play football. I told him, "Maybe I should get a fresh start somewhere else."

He told me to play balls-out the rest of the year and we'd talk when the season was over. He also told me he couldn't get much for me in a trade at that point anyway. *That* pissed me off. Perhaps the biggest proof that I was back and one of the games I'm proudest of came a few weeks later on a Sunday night in New Orleans. I played with a bad shoulder—a torn pectoral muscle. I shouldn't have had my uniform on, but we had to have that game. Harry was out and Carl Banks was out and Phil was out. I had to have my marketing guy Steve Rosner help me get my shirt and coat on during the week.

They strapped this leather harness on me and I could only lift my arm up a little more than waist-high. Basically I was playing with one arm. The pain wasn't bad once the shoulder was still, but every time I tried to tackle somebody, I felt stupid, because after every hit, I was doubled over with pain, down on my knees. "Fix it," I kept telling our trainer. "But I'm not coming out of the game."

Perry Williams, one of our corners, would put his hands on his knees and let me lean on him in the huddle. The pain was so bad that there were tears in my eyes and I had to grit my teeth. "You all right?" Perry kept asking me, and I kept saying, "Just let me be."

JOHN WASHINGTON

In the huddle, I noticed LT would grimace. He said, "Let's make some plays and get me out of here." It inspired us. We would have to play even harder; we had to do more than we could just to help him and get him off the field.

We won the game—somehow—and I had three sacks, somehow, and two forced fumbles. After the game, Bill put his forehead against mine and said, "You were great tonight." And I said, "I don't know how I got through it." Mighta been tears in his eyes and tears in my eyes, too.

BILL PARCELLS

There are only a few times you get a chance to talk to a player where it's just him and you. Those are the kind of things you remember. I remember that moment with him. (Chuckle) I wasn't too lavish with the *"greats."*

Steve Rosner met me by the team bus and I told him, "I can't get my coat on, but I don't want you to do it in front of everybody. Let's go off to the side so you can help me." The team really appreciated what I did and they were saying all kinds of nice things about me on the way home. I didn't hear a lot of it, though. I took my pain pills and slept like a baby the entire plane ride back to Newark.

MYRON GUYTON, Giants safety

The first thing I learned from LT was that there was no such thing as being injured. If you can walk, you can play. When LT was out with his torn Achilles was a perfect example. We were losing at halftime. LT had a cast on, but he came into the locker room and took off his street clothes

and put on his uniform and said, "If you guys don't want to play, fuck it, I'll go out and play."

Some guys play with a sore toe and want a medal. For me, pain doesn't enter into my game plan. That's football. I played with a fractured ankle in 1989, thanks to a cut block by tight end Wesley Walls in a Monday-night game in San Francisco. I was screaming in agony as I was carted off the field. The official diagnosis was a hairline fracture at the base of the right tibia. Whatever they called it, it hurt like hell. My teammates were furious at the cheap shot, and worried about me when they saw me on the ground wailing, "I blew out my knee! It's over! It's over!"

Of course, it wasn't over. Dr. Russell Warren, the Giants' orthopedist, told me late in the week that if he saw me limping the morning of the Eagles game, he wouldn't let me play. They wouldn't shoot me up, so I went and got some DMSO, an anti-inflammatory they use on horses, from some contacts at the racetrack across from Giants Stadium. Then, since I didn't want to wear a brace, I told Ronnie Barnes, "Just tape it up as tight as you can." Dr. Warren let me play when he saw that I could get up on my toes and walk on my heels.

I was in for fifteen plays against the Eagles. In those fifteen plays, I had seven tackles. That was a lot of pain. Bill once said that he'd put my strength of will up against anyone's, and while that helped me in football, it probably hurt me in my fight against cocaine. I wanted the Giants to shoot me up for the game the next week in Denver and threatened to find my own guy if they wouldn't. Dr. Warren didn't believe in that shit. Finally, Ronnie Barnes flew this podiatrist in from Los Angeles. He escorted me to a room away from the locker room area and gave me a numbing shot.

I played. End of story.

CHAPTER EIGHT

Around this time, I was getting pretty tired of giving bars and restaurants all my money, so I started thinking about opening my own place, LT's. My partners had big plans, and it wasn't costing me anything. (Well, it wasn't *supposed* to be costing me anything.)

MARK LEPSELTER, manager

LT acted like a host, walking around greeting people, making sure they were happy and being taken care of. One night he goes up to a woman who's kind of heavyset. "How you doin', darling?" he asks her. They're making small talk and then he says, "Hey, are you pregnant?" She gets really annoyed at this and says, "No!" But LT is so charismatic that he recovered beautifully. Without batting an eye, he says to her, "You wanna be?"

It was good, in the beginning. It was a fun place to be, especially Thursday, Friday, Saturday nights, and Sundays after the game. It was a meat market. I was getting them out of there by the dozen. Without the drugs, I hadn't really changed. I partied as hard as ever, just within what was "acceptable" to the team and the league. And, as it turns out, there's plenty of wiggle room.

I also had a piece of a strip joint called First & Ten on Route 17, behind Giants Stadium. I used to open it for my teammates, call the strippers in, and we'd party all night. As long as we locked the doors and didn't let anybody else in, it was like a private party and the cops would leave us alone. And being the gracious host that I am, I also used to throw parties at my house all the time. I used to send Linda away on trips so that the guys would feel comfortable. I remember one time in training camp, when it was brutally hot and the coaches told us that we didn't have practice the next day, Saturday. Within two hours of that announcement, a teammate and I put together a pool party at my house that was OUTstanding. Every player could bring one guy . . . and five women. One guy and five women. One of the greatest pool parties I've ever ever seen. Bitches everywhere. About half the team was there. It was wild. Regardless of where I was—home or away—I wouldn't stop partying until the sun came up.

PHIL SIMMS, Giants quarterback

I'm in a quarterbacks' meeting getting a cup of coffee and Lawrence walks in at two minutes to nine, wearing leather pants, a big leather jacket, sunglasses on. He takes the

sunglasses off and I start to laugh, and he starts to laugh. I say, "You're just coming in from the night, aren't you?"

He says, "I haven't even been home." We're laughing hysterically now. He says, "There's only one way I'm going to get through practice today—I'm just going to go crazy," and that's what he did. He got some coffee and started talking trash and got real upbeat. At practice, he was screaming and yelling like a madman. Nobody could block him.

There were plenty of practices when I knew I had no business being out there. I used to go to our trainer, and say, "Ronnie, what have you got in that box of yours? Whatcha got for me?" We had like a big whirlpool with cold, cold water. I'd put my head under that bad boy and keep it under just to clear my head. I learned that from the old guys—Van Pelt, Brian Kelley—who had mastered the art of recovering from hangovers.

You might say I was addicted to speed, too. I loved driving, and I can't even begin to tell you how many cars I went through. I guess I've always driven the way I lived—in the fast lane. And it ain't for the faint of heart.

CARL BANKS

We're in training camp [1984], probably fifteen minutes before bed check. It's raining out, but he says, "C'mon, rookie, ride with me." We get in his BMW 850, and we're swerving through White Plains 'cause he had to have a specific type of Skoal, and the closest spot didn't have it, so he's zipping all over town and he's fishtailing. It was the scariest experience I ever had. Just to get a can of chew.

I like the raw stuff, fine-cut chewing tobacco. You know those Surgeon General warnings: You Might Get Cancer? Hell, no. I want the shit that says, You damn sure *will* get it. I also scared holy hell out of Jim Burt one time when I went 140 mph through the tollbooth on the Garden State Parkway on our way from the golf course to a banquet.

PHIL SIMMS

We were going to Pine Valley to play golf. Lawrence showed up late and it looked like he had had a pretty good night. He wanted to drive, so Jim Burt and I argued over who was going to be in the backseat because we figured we'd have a better chance of surviving in the backseat with a seat belt on. Jim's bigger than me, so he got the backseat. Lawrence takes off down the [New Jersey] Turnpike. We're going about 100 mph and I'm saying, over and over again, "Omigod! Omigod!"

After about thirty minutes, a car pulls up beside us. This big guy puts his police hat on and yells over his loudspeaker, "HEY! SLOW DOWN!"

Lawrence gives him a wave, like "Yeah, yeah, thanks." And goes even faster.

Of course, the cop let me get away. Speaking of Burt, I would see him on Route 17 on our way to Giants Stadium and race him there. I had a new Mercedes, but I didn't care. I'd go over curbs and shit, or on the shoulder. I even cut Burt off. But that's what he gets for trying to beat me in a daggone Toyota Corolla.

Tolls were a real bitch. You had to stop for them? That's just plain crazy.

VICKI COREY, my administrative assistant

Lawrence was driving on the Garden State Parkway and I handed him change for the toll. So he picks up speed all of a sudden and flips the change. The only problem was the window was closed, and the change bounced off the window. He tells me, "I don't pay tolls. When I get home, I'll write 'em a check."

Another time, I was late to catch the team plane for a road trip, so I was on the Turnpike doing 100 mph on the shoulder. I wasn't even going to stop for a cop. I drove my new Porsche up the ramp at Newark Airport, got to the gate, and jumped out of the car. I gave the skycap $100, threw him the keys, and said, "I'm Lawrence Taylor. Just park it somewhere and send the keys to the stadium."

MIKE POPE, Giants tight ends coach

A number of times we would watch him drive his car to the airport when we were leaving for a trip. He'd park right in front of the terminal. They'd tow his car, and when we came back he'd just pay the fifty bucks to get the car out.

I bought a Jaguar from Brad Benson and it kept overheating. Brad, who owned a top-rate Jaguar dealership, kept telling me no other car had the same problem. "This car's junk; you have to take it back and fix it!" I would tell him.

He'd have his people look at it and tell me, "There's nothing wrong with it."

BRAD BENSON, Giants left tackle

I finally figured out what the problem was: During summer training camp he used to leave the car running with the windows up and the air-conditioning on full-blast when he went to get lunch, so that it would be cool when he came out. He says, "If I can't leave my car running during lunch, then I don't want it!"

Not surprisingly, that car didn't last too long for me anyway. I was driving that Jag to a club one night, doing 80 miles per hour, when I hit the guardrail. *Bam!* Totaled the car. I got out of the Jaguar, flagged down the first car that came down the road. It happened to be a limo. I said, "Listen, take me to this club."

I partied all night at that club, then called a tow truck when the club closed. Really really late now. Tow truck picks me up, picks my Jag up, and drops me off at the stadium for work the next morning.

Most of the time I had the perfect plan for making the plane on time.

CARL BANKS

He would tell us, "The secret is to pack your clothes on Friday night, put 'em in the trunk of your car, then go out, and then don't go home. Just park in the stadium parking lot. Tell somebody to knock on your window when it's time to come in for the Saturday-morning meeting."

After Friday's practice, he would ask, "Okay, who's going to be here early? If you see my car out there, tap on my window." That plan worked for a lot of us.

I'd also keep some clothes in my locker for convenience's sake.

CARL BANKS

He always kept five changes of clothes in his locker for those occasions before road trips when he stayed out all night, and he'd come right from the club to the stadium. He'd be so out of it that whatever he put on didn't match a lick. Or the shit he had piled up in his locker wasn't quite up to par to put on. He'd have on a winter overcoat, a sports jacket wrinkled beyond recognition . . . and no shirt. Many a time he was so out of it when he'd get dressed that his shoes didn't match. Or he would end up putting on a pair of turf shoes with no socks with a suit and get on the plane. He'd walk up and down the aisle of the plane trying to find somebody who had extra shoes or an extra shirt.

It was almost a transient lifestyle. I mean, anything to stay busy, to keep moving. I'd always feel that if I stopped, if I paused for a second, then the Enemy, the coke, would rise up. And I couldn't have that, no sir.

We had a great 1989 season, going 12–4. But then we lost to the L.A. Rams in OT, 19–13. I had another good year—fifteen sacks, another Pro Bowl—and now I was like, hey, when am I getting mine?

So I held out for forty-four days before the '90 season, until the Giants paid me better than the Eagles were paying their defensive stud, Reggie White. I thought my Giant days were over. I felt I was getting shafted making only $950,000. I wanted $3 million a year. If we had had the same free agent system that's in the NFL today, the sky would have been the limit for me. The Giants had offered me $1.2 million. We ended up working out a deal for three years, $7.5 million, the largest deal in NFL history for a defensive player.

JOE COURREGE, the agent who got me my final contract

George Young said that nobody would want Lawrence Taylor. Nobody would trade for him. And I was able to chal-

lenge that statement. He said, "You go try." I said, "Will you give me permission to go trade him?" So he gives me a letter that said I had permission to go try to trade him. I won't say he erred, but the fact he gave me that letter to go shop Lawrence Taylor opened a Pandora's box. I can remember walking around with a copy of the letter on Giants stationery with permission to go shop Lawrence Taylor. It was like a key to opening up a bank vault. Without that letter, nobody would have talked to me.

LT's instructions were simple: Make me the highest-paid defensive player. So I got on a train and went down to Philadelphia and walked into [then Eagles GM] Harry Gamble's office, and he couldn't believe I had the letter. He said, "This is serious." I said, "This is dead serious." We began to talk turkey, and somehow it got released to the Philadelphia media; the next day there was a big full-page article about it. I told Harry Gamble that if you make the right offer, the Giants will not match it, and you'll end up with a bonanza deal and a sellout every week. Harry Gamble was very excited about it.

I also called the Houston Oilers and asked them if they would have any interest and they said absolutely, they sure would. But it would have been a three-way transaction involving Minnesota. The Giants had right of first refusal, and so we got Young's attention.

LT really began to get antsy—he wanted to play, yet he wanted that money. We just had to go to the wire, where we compromised on the deal. And four days before the Monday-night opener against the Eagles, LT signed.

After the contract was settled, I walked in on Bill's regular Wednesday press conference and announced, "I'm home!"

In the '90 opener, I had two and a half sacks against the Eagles, and eleven tackles. That was all adrenaline. You know me; I don't do no off-season workout. And now, of course, I had another reason to celebrate—and lots more money to spend. I threw a couple parties at First & Ten that seemed to be particularly memorable to my teammates after a couple of long flights back from the West Coast in November and December.

ERIC DORSEY

LT personally came up to me on the plane and made sure I was going. A young lady working at his club specifically asked for me to show up. I was glad I did because I fell in love [that night].

It was like something out of a movie. Lionel Manuel was the DJ. Maurice Carthon was the bartender. And all the rest of us were patrons. One night LT didn't have the key to open the club, so he had to use a crowbar. He broke into his own club. The cops showed up; I guess the alarm went off. It was all cool; it was his place.

The next day he calls my home early, six-thirty, seven in the morning; I guess he hadn't been to sleep yet. "Eric, is everything okay? How'd everything go with the girl?" He was checking up on everybody to make sure everybody was okay and had gotten home safe. I guess he felt responsible. A lot of the wives were really pissed off at

him. Some of the wives were really mad and I think he said if any wives say anything, just blame everything on him.

WILLIAM ROBERTS

Everybody was jamming and drinking. There were a lot of lap dances going on. There were women on stage and five or six in the back and LT was trying to screw all of them.

Finally, we won the Super Bowl again that year. We weren't the steamrollers we'd been the last time, though. This time we had to fight for everything we got, especially after Phil Simms injured his foot on December 15 against the Bills and Jeff Hostetler had to come to the rescue. Jeff led us to five straight victories and another championship. That surprised people, because Phil was such an important player for us, but defenses were used to our quarterback sitting back in the pocket. Now we had a guy who could run the ball. I didn't think Jeff could win us a championship, but I thought he could win us some games. He surprised me. Third-and-six, third-and-seven, he was able to pull that ball down and run for some big first downs. He was able to move the chains. Hell, he probably surprised himself.

That year's NFC championship game in San Francisco was the greatest game I ever played in because of the stakes and the competitiveness and the greatness of the opponent. We were going against the mighty San Francisco 49ers, who had Joe Montana, Jerry Rice, Roger Craig, Ronnie Lott, and their latest genius coach, George Seifert.

Everyone expected the 49ers to beat us, and then three-peat as champions . . . until Erik Howard jarred the ball loose from Craig and I recovered it at our forty-three-yard line with about two and a half minutes left to set up Matt Bahr's game-winning field goal.

RONNIE LOTT, 49ers Hall of Fame safety

He played the game the way Butkus played the game, but he played as if the rpm of a record was off the charts. He played so much faster than Butkus. I don't think people realize the destructiveness he brought to the game. I'd never seen that kind of nastiness, all-out, 100 percent, for four quarters. He was gonna come after you and he was gonna punish you.

I had always told Bill that we would win two Super Bowls together, and on the flight from San Francisco to Super Bowl XXV, I was so excited I started dialing random Tampa phone numbers. As I'm running up and down the aisle of the plane, I'm screaming into my cell phone, "This is LT. We're comin' down there to kick ass!"

Of course, I managed to squeeze in some leisure time in Tampa. Imagine my delight when the bus pulled up to the team hotel and right across the street was the famous Tanga Lounge, one of the homes of the lap dance. Now you know by now what a stickler Bill was about us having no distractions. I just had to yell out, "Well, Bill, looks like you didn't think of *everything!* I know where we're going tonight!"

Bill had told us before the playoffs, "You guys get me to the Super Bowl, and I'll show you how to win the Super Bowl." So in the first meeting during Super Bowl week, Bill walked up the aisle and was about to address the team when I stood up and said, "Well?!?!"

And Bill said, "Well, *what?*"

I said, "Well, we got you here. Now what the hell are you going to do to help us win this game against these Buffalo Bills?"

Bill laughed, and said, "I always hold up my end of the bargain. You guys are going to read a lot of things from my mouth this week in the press. Don't believe a word. I'm going to blow so much smoke up Buffalo's skirts all week. Let 'em start believing how good they are."

So that's what we all did. All week, we told the media, "Shucks, Buffalo is so good," and "Golly, we just hope we represent the NFC well," and what a juggernaut Buffalo is, etc.

A few days before the game, there was a picture of seven or eight of the Bills in a jewelry store in the *Tampa Tribune*. They were getting sized for their Super Bowl rings! Bill showed us that and said, "We got 'em, boys! They're believing their own press clippings. We got 'em."

Another day, practice was dragging, so Bill asked me to start a fight with Jumbo Elliott during the nine-on-seven drills. Off the field, Jumbo was our mild-mannered offensive left tackle. But he was mean on the field, and had a short fuse. I started talking a little smack, and gave him extra smacks, and *boom!* It was on. The fight was a doozy, too—it took half the team to separate us. But it fired the team up. It sure as hell fired Jumbo up—he kicked Bruce Smith's ass all night in the Super Bowl.

Jumbo was my teammate, which means there was never anything personal in that fight. In fact, that same night, Jumbo, Erik Howard, Steve DeOssie, and I went to this "upscale gentlemen's establishment." We were having a couple of "sodas" when in walk some of the Bills' star players— Jim Kelly, Thurman Thomas, Cornelius Bennett, Darryl Talley, and Bruce Smith. They sit about twenty feet away from us. Bruce Smith was wearing this big chain around his neck with a big gold BRUCE, and a blazer with no shirt. So I get up and scream, "Sonsabitches! Jumbo's going to kick your ass, Bruce!" Jumbo was tugging on me, trying to get me to sit down so Bruce wouldn't get riled up.

Belichick found a way to disrupt the Bills' fast-paced offense—he told us it wouldn't be the worst thing in the world if we accidentally kicked the ball once in a while after the officials placed it down on the line of scrimmage. That was to slow down Buffalo's no-huddle offense. Erik Howard must have kicked the ball three or four times after the referee set it. That wasn't the only slowdown tactic we used. Guys would unpile slower than Bill could run the forty. Guys would jump on piles long after the tackle had been made so that it would take even longer to unpile 'em. It screwed the Bills up, yes it did. So if you're going to ask me if I'm surprised Belichick won the Super Bowl in 2001 with the Patriots, the answer is no.

Super Bowl XXV wasn't like the '86 Super Bowl, when we were a dominant team. We had to scrap, scratch, and claw, man. The play I remember most from Super Bowl XXV was late in the game, when we were facing fourth and long, and Mark Ingram caught the ball in the right flat. He was four yards short of the first down when two guys grabbed him, but he kicked, and he pushed, and he hopped, and he got across that first-down marker.

The game came down to the final seconds. We were clinging to a 20–19 lead. At that point in my career, I wasn't on the field goal block team, but when Scott Norwood lined up for that forty-seven-yard field goal, I was on that field. I told the guy who usually comes in for me on field goals, "I ain't leavin'."

I had to be a part of this play—it's the worst thing in the world to be sitting on the sidelines and watching somebody try to beat you. Especially a damn kicker. Also, I really thought that I could make a difference. I thought I was going to block that kick. I said to myself, "This is like an LT moment." They snapped the ball, and I dove. It wasn't an LT moment.

The kick went up, and I was on the ground facefirst. I didn't look up. Instead, I looked at Erik Howard. He was on his butt looking back, watching the kick while I was on my stomach, just looking at him. I didn't want to see it.

It was wide right. "Oh, yeah!"

I remembered that Bill had said earlier that day, "If we win this thing, I want to ride off this field." So now I'm jumping up and down, celebrating, and I holler at Carl Banks, "Let's go, baby. We have to give the coach a ride."

As we carried him off the field with all those lights flashing and everyone whooping and hollering, I had no idea that this was the beginning of the end of my football career.

CHAPTER NINE

Bill left the Giants four months after Super Bowl XXV. He'd told me a week or two before the game that this was it. I just listened. It was sad. I always thought we would leave together.

I couldn't see how George Young and the organization could allow him to go. But I could see the power struggle. As for me, I didn't want to come back, but I did. Somebody told me a long time ago—give 'em ten of your best, and make 'em take two of your worst. I really didn't have the drive to play—I had lost the will to hit. I didn't want to be out there. Bill was my number one motivator. When shit wasn't goin' right, and I wasn't playing right, he always had a way to get me excited about playing the game. When Ray Handley became our coach, though, it took me a while to get up mentally for practice. It was the first time in ten years I hadn't walked onto a football field and had Bill hitting me with snide remarks.

I knew the Giants weren't getting back to any more Super

Bowls after Bill left—at least not anytime soon. It wasn't strictly that the new guy was a bad coach. It was more that we, like a lot of teams, didn't handle success well. A lot of egos blew up after that Super Bowl win. The same thing happened after our first Super Bowl—*everybody* started writing books. Even me.

After Parcells left for television and Belichick left for the head coaching job with the Cleveland Browns, Handley took over and named Rod Rust the defensive coordinator. There were some problems there. We had a veteran defensive unit, one that had just won a Super Bowl, and we didn't like his read-and-react defensive philosophy much. Early in the season, we were getting killed in the first half by the Cowboys.

STEVE DeOSSIE

I was in charge of calling our defensive signals. At halftime LT comes over to me and says, "When I give you the signal, call Stack Cover 2." We had won the Super Bowl with that defense the year before, but I tell him, "It's not even in the package."

He says, "I don't give a shit. Look around. Everybody on this defense knows it. We can play Stack Cover 2."

So we're in the huddle early in the second half and LT gives me the sign. I say, "Okay, guys, Stack Cover 2." Everyone thought I was crazy. "Relax," I said. "We can play this defense." And lo and behold, we start playing Giant defense again. But I know that everything we do is on film, and will be scrutinized by the coaches, so I try to cover up this mutiny by making all these exaggerated, ridiculous hand gestures, pointing to this guy, pointing to that guy, like I was moving people around on my own. I probably looked like I was having an epileptic fit.

In the film room the next day, LT and I are on the floor in the front, in our usual spots. When the game film comes to the second half, Rust says to me, "What are you calling here?" And I give him the closest thing in our current playbook to Stack Cover 2 and tell him that I had audiblized to blah-blah-blah. Rust asks me why and I say, "I probably saw something."

I look over at LT, expecting him to help me out, but he doesn't say a damn thing. He's just trying not to bust out laughing. We go to the next play and the next play and the next play and Rust keeps asking me why I called this or that, and I'm making shit up, like, "I saw something in the guard's eye," or . . . Finally, after about the sixth time I do this, Rust says, "Let me guess: You saw something . . ." LT just left me twisting in the wind.

And I wasn't even getting paid a coach's salary! I regretted letting Ray talk me out of retiring. He said, "We got an opportunity to keep something special going," and blah-blah-blah. I talked to Bill, who said Ray was an offensive mastermind. Some mastermind. Ray lasted two years, and I think those two years set the Giants back a hundred years. No one I know defended Handley.

He wasn't a strong coach. The players started fighting with him almost immediately. There were eleven chiefs and

no Indians. Handley had gotten into something that he couldn't control. Everybody was doing their own thing. No discipline whatsoever. It was complete chaos. Guys dissed Handley behind his back, and to his face.

I was there when Ray and Carl Banks went at it in the locker room at halftime once. I was out with my Achilles injury and Carl actually had Ray up between the lockers, and I had to pull Carl off of him. Carl and I had words and I screamed, "Are you crazy? That's your boss!"

COREY MILLER

Carl is just irate: "I'm tired of this fucking shit. The coaches suck. They're not letting us play." We hear this loud noise. Carl had Ray Handley two-gapped up against the wall, just screaming at him and going off on him. LT comes around the corner from the trainer's room, he's got that big-ass boot on and says, "Carl, what the fuck are you doing? You can't do this shit!" Lawrence was pulling Carl off Ray Handley. Everybody's gotta restrain those two.

CARL BANKS

There was a lot of bitching going on in the meeting room. It got pretty boisterous in there. I got up and left to get my back rubbed because I was having back spasms. Ray was kinda coming in on the tail end of all the bullshit. He said, "Where the fuck are you going?" I said, "I have to get some heat rubbed into my back, I'm having back spasms."

He said, "Get your ass back in the meeting room." I said, "Coach, I gotta go get my back rubbed." He grabbed me—LT and those guys didn't see that—and tried to jerk me by the arm back to the meeting room. When he did that, I pushed him up against the wall. Lawrence rushed out of the meeting room and said, "What are you doing?" I said, "This fucking guy put his hand on me." Lawrence and I were screaming—I don't think it was one of those situations where we had to be separated to the point we were gonna punch each other.

Ray should have suspended Carl, but nothing happened to him. Carl's a good friend, but I didn't like the way that whole thing was handled. I lost respect for Ray. I had tried to be an ally to him, but then he lost my respect. It was a bad situation. I myself would never have tolerated anything like it. If anyone disrespected me, they would pay for it, like this rookie tight end did during training camp.

JOEY SMITH, Giants wide receiver

The offense was giving LT and the defense a look, and I was in the huddle. LT was in a laid-back mood, with his chinstrap unbuckled and his shoes untied. One of the offensive veterans decided to play a joke on the rookie Derek Brown. He told him, "You gotta hit LT!" Phil Simms said, "Don't touch LT!" But Brown needed to make an early impression, so he hits LT full speed, and the guys were yelling "Oh yeah!"

> When LT buckles his chin strap and ties his shoes, it's a live practice. That means he's ticked off. Ray Handley was the coach at the time. He ran over to LT and said, "It's not a live practice." LT didn't say a word.
>
> Phil Simms knew what was coming, and left the huddle. In stepped Kent Graham. The next snap LT hit Derek Brown with some kind of head body slap and broke his nose. Brown was dazed and watched the rest of practice. When practice was over, his football helmet had no face mask. LT had busted it. You don't mess with LT.

There was some disrespecting going on that I couldn't do anything about, though: the zebras were constantly dissing me. In our first game of the Handley era, a Monday-nighter at home, the offensive linemen for the 49ers were holding and choking and mugging me, but the officials never called anything. I wasn't getting the respect superstars are supposed to get. I felt like the football version of Charles Barkley, who never got the calls that Jordan got.

Needless to say, the season went directly into the shitter. We went from champs to chumps, with a measly 8–8 record. As each week passed, I missed Bill more and more. Bill was more than a coach to me. He was a friend. A big brother. There was never a dull moment with Bill. Even in my tenth year, his last year as the Giants coach, I still had a fire in my gut, because Bill had ways to keep me interested in the game. When Bill almost took the Tampa Bay job after the 1991 season, I would have been a Buc. Bill and I had always said that when he goes, I go. And if I go, he goes.

DAVE MEGGETT, Giants running back

LT's relationship with Bill was the way I wanted to be with my head coach. They were like brothers and friends, and Bill was also a mentor and a father figure. That was a beautiful relationship that those guys had. They would talk all the time. During practice, after practice, breakfast, lunch, dinner. In the locker room; on the plane. It seemed like it was 24/7 those two were always talking.

And, for some reason, I missed his bitchiness. Once when we were practicing like shit one time, Bill screamed, "I'm not wasting my coaches' time. You guys don't want to get coached today. Coach yourselves. You guys know everything." He walked off the practice field and took his assistants with him.

Simms and I reckoned that we knew what the hell to do, so we decided to run practice ourselves. Simms ran the offense, I ran the defense. But first I locked the gate.

STEVE DeOSSIE

After about thirty, forty minutes, a couple of the assistant coaches started straggling back and were peering through the fence, which is about eight feet high. Then about ten minutes later, here comes Bill. "Hey," he screams, "unlock this fucking gate!"

Ed Wagner, our equipment man, looks over at LT, who screams, "No! I wanna see that fat bastard climb the

fence." Then he yells to Parcells: "We don't need you. We got a good practice going here. We don't need no stupid coaches. I don't even know if we're going to let you guys make the trip this week!"

LT finally let Parcells in, and we went on to have a great practice, and won the game.

Before one Redskins game, Bill was ranting and raving and just being a real asshole—he always had *something* to say to *everybody*, you know?

BILL PARCELLS

He used to stand next to me during the National Anthem. We both were a little superstitious. He liked playing the Redskins, especially down there. He was pretty high-strung, he was kinda pacing a little. I could always tell when he was a little nervous. He couldn't stand still. I hadn't said too much to him all week, but I had been on quite a few players. Right after the National Anthem ends, I just turned and yelled, "Are you gonna play today?" And he yelled right back at me, "Just worry about those other SOBs you coach!"

I used to get bored a lot in practice, so Bill would get some poor rookie offensive lineman to rattle my cage. One day it was a gung-ho kid trying to make an impression—cutting me and hitting me after the whistle and shit like that. Finally, enough was enough, and I started kicking his ass and beating up on any offensive player they threw in front of me.

Here's how bored I would get: During the offensive drills I used to take the blocking dummies over to the side and line them up and tackle them. Sometimes I'd even talk to them.

I'll always remember a film session my rookie year where Bill kept going on about Hugh Green. Later, it was Pat Swilling, who happened to wear number 56 for the Saints. Sometimes Bill would ride me by saying that Swilling was the New King of number 56. He'd say all the kids wanted to wear number 56 because of Swilling. That shit would rile me up.

I think it was in 1989 before a game against the Vikings that Bill started calling me "Whatsthematterwith?" He'd say, "Lawrence, I'm going to change your name to Whatsthematterwith? 'cause that's all I hear from the press: 'What's the matter with Taylor?'" Then he said, "You're gettin' old. You can't do it no more. We should just put you out to pasture and shoot you!"

Bill knew how to push my hot button. Before Bill addressed the team after that game, I stood up and said, "Well, they ain't going to ask you 'What's the matter with Taylor?' Not after they see the film of that game!"

JOHNNY PARKER

Parcells and Taylor both understood that deep down inside, despite Lawrence's cool, maybe even nonchalant exterior, he wanted to win. Parcells didn't try to put Lawrence in a box. He didn't try to make him conform, and I think Lawrence appreciated that.

Bill knew I was never a me guy, and he always used to tell people, "With Lawrence, it was always, 'Did we win and who do we play next?' Some guys never understood that this is a team game. When Handley was the coach, we came into the locker room one time after getting our asses kicked in the first half. One of the defensive backs says, "I had *my* man covered."

I grabbed him by the jersey and slammed him up against the wall and said loudly and clearly: "Your man is the man with the ball! The man with the ball scored." I thought he was going to have a heart attack. All he said was, "Yup. Yup. Yup."

BYRON HUNT

There was no better team player than Lawrence Taylor. LT moved to inside linebacker to replace Harry Carson in '83. He was getting beat up by everybody. I remember him shaking his head and saying, "This is a tough position to play." But I've never ever heard him say, "No, I'm not gonna do that." He played on special teams coverage as a rookie. When Lawrence split out wide, they had to put two guys on him, and he would beat the double team, and the guy would fair-catch it all the time because he was so afraid of getting hit by LT.

BILL PARCELLS

He responded to competition. All you had to do was show him where it was.

And competition could be anywhere, doing anything. Phil Simms and I used to get into arguments over who could do the other's job better. One day I said to him, "I can throw this football farther than your ass could ever throw it."

He said, "Give me a break."

I promptly threw that sonuvabitch into the second level at Giants Stadium. Phil didn't even bother trying. Dan Dierdorf once challenged me to throw it up into the third tier, and I did that, too. Hey, maybe I missed my true calling.

O. J. Simpson—my old colleague from an HBO show we did together—bet that I couldn't knock a golf ball out of Giants Stadium with my driver. He gave me three shots. I put the first ball down under the goalpost, right where the tunnel is, and knocked that bad boy out of the opposite end of the stadium.

Even children would be shown no mercy!

GUS ORNSTEIN, my friend Steve's son

LT would not allow me to go to bed until he beat me in Nintendo. We'd stay up until two in the morning while my mother was yelling at me. LT would not let my mother put me in bed: "He's not going to bed until I beat him!" I was so tired I finally had to let him beat me so I could go to bed.

So yeah, I liked competition. And nothing could compare to Sundays. My thing was make them adjust to you instead of you adjusting to them. Defense has always been a . . . what do they teach you? React? Fuck react. Let them react to us. Blitzing is the only defensive weapon that the offense has to react to. The offense had better worry about what I was going to do. There aren't many situations in life where I'm in complete control. Not even in my own house. But put me on a football field, and there's nothing I can't handle.

CARL BANKS

We were in a pass-rush meeting with Lamar Leachman, our defensive-line coach. Lawrence traditionally gets to practice just on time. Or a little after, like he did on this day. We're in our second meeting and Lawrence walks in. He's clearly feeling the effects of the night before, so he sits down, pulls his shirt over his head, and falls asleep. Out cold.

He wakes up when there are just two plays left on the film. Out of the clear blue, Leachman, who knows that Lawrence has been asleep, calls on him to diagram a play. Well, Lawrence gets up and diagrams all of our pass-rush schemes for the game. He says, "Right end does this, left end does this, inside rush should be this . . ."

Lamar, in his good-ol'-boy drawl, says: "Goddamn, boy, how'd you figure that out? Weren't you asleep up under there?" And we all busted up laughing, because we knew we'd just had a visitation from the Genius.

I don't know about genius, but by this point in my career, I knew all the tricks and playing was as easy as breathing. My bread and butter was always the speed rush, and timing was critical for it to work, so you'd have to look for clues. For instance, sometimes a quarterback will give a little indication when that ball was going to be snapped, which gave me an extra jump off the ball. Joe Montana, just before he snapped the ball, always looked at the center's back. He looks at the center's back, and I'm gone. I picked that up on film after years of playing him.

JOE MONTANA,
49ers Hall of Fame quarterback

LT was one of those unique kind of guys who had quickness, strength, and speed. You were damned if you did and damned if you didn't. So you couldn't run at him and you couldn't run away from him. You watched video, and he would run around tackles, run over them, run around backs and outquick them, or bowl them over like they were nothing. You had to be leery where he was all the time.

By now, the years had added up. In fact, I planned on retiring in 1992. But, of course, nothing goes like it should and I tore my Achilles.

CHAPTER TEN

I'll never forget that day—November 8, in a game we lost to the Packers. I came around the corner and leaped to knock down a Brett Favre pass. I hit the ball, and then I hit the ground. I knew that ball was nearby, though, like a pop-up, and I thought I could catch it. As I sprung up, though, I got jerked down by somebody and my tendon snapped.

COREY MILLER

There was silence in the stadium. People were shocked because he was such a warrior. "LT? Come on! He can't get hurt!"

JOHNNY PARKER

To me, it was almost like when you saw Larry Holmes battering Muhammad Ali. You just knew somebody you had seen be so great, and somebody you thought was practically invincible, was now no longer that. It was just sad to see such a warrior carried off, and you thought then it would probably be the end. I think he came back so he could walk off. He didn't want to leave Giants Stadium on a cart.

When I was lying there on the ground, I could feel a little burn, the size of a dime, and then the whole ankle felt like it was in flames. As soon as it popped, I knew I was in trouble. When Ronnie Barnes and Dr. Warren ran out to me, I was screaming, "It's gone!" and I was crying. "My career is over!" I don't remember Ronnie Barnes saying anything to me. But I did hear one of them say, "Let's get a cart for you."

No way Giant fans were going to see me carted off the field, so I said, "I'm going to walk off." But Superman had lost his cape. I couldn't walk. Banks and Erik Howard lifted me onto a flatbed cart. As I rode off the field, the fans chanted "LT! LT! LT!" I'm sure they were wondering if they would ever see me wearing number 56 again. I was wondering the same damn thing.

That night, drinking my patented scotch and milk at LT's, I had tears in my eyes when I told Rosner, "I'm not sure I can beat this one."

Bill came to visit the next day and we talked about old times and had a few laughs and so did Harry Carson, who told me that no one would hold it against me if I changed my mind about retiring. He also mentioned that the last thing I wanted to do when I was fifty years old was regret that I had left the game while I still had more to give.

I was the Giants number one draft pick. This is me on opening day at Giants training camp, doing my thing, while my new teammates looked on. They look kinda awed, don't they?

David F. Austin Photography, courtesy of Linda Taylor

There's nothing like running out onto the field, with the crowd screaming, "LT! LT! LT!"

Marrying my college sweetheart, Linda, was one of the best days of my life—and one of the smartest things I ever did.

I'll never forget the game on November 15, 1985. In the second quarter, I knocked into Redskin quarterback Joe Theismann, breaking both the bones in his leg. He never played football again.

Me and my sweet family:

With Tanisha at home in New Jersey,

trying to cut T. J.'s hair,

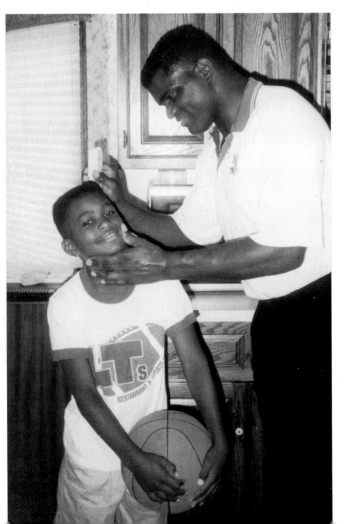

and the five of us on a family trip to SeaWorld.

T.J., Paula, me, Tanisha, and Whitney celebrating Tanisha's graduation in 2002.

Me and Bill Parcells, the coach of coaches, December 1989: We had just clinched the NFC East Championship, and couldn't be happier.

Our last dance, at Paul's wedding, 1991. I was best man, but I was miserable. I had a wife with an ass like Jennifer Lopez and I screwed up and lost her.

AP/Wide World Photos

Moments after I tore my Achilles tendon while trying to nail Green Bay's Brett Favre on November 8, 1992. It messed up my retirement plans.

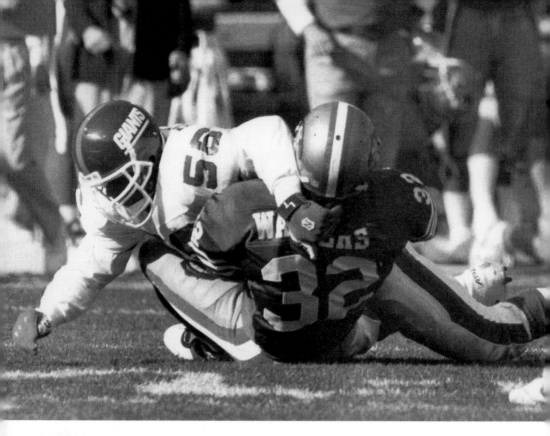

Stopping San Francisco's Ricky Watters (number 32) on January 15, 1994, the last game I played as a Giant.

And then I left the field for the last time at Candlestick Park. You already know what I was thinking about next.

After the game, I announced my retirement. After Phil Simms gave me a hug, I almost lost it.

New York Post/Bob Olen

On Monday, October 10, 1994, they retired my jersey in front of my fans at Giants Stadium.

My parents, Clarence and Iris, were there with me that day.

New York Post/Bob Olen

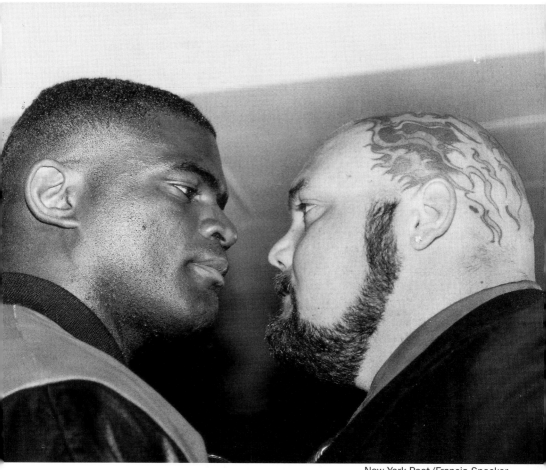

New York Post/Francis Specker

Wrestler Bam Bam Bigelow and I at the Harley-Davidson Café in New York City, announcing our upcoming match in February 1995. To relieve the tension, I gave Bam Bam a big wet one.

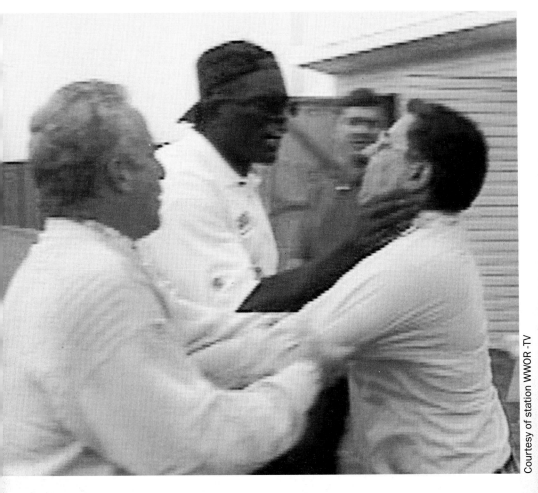

September 1995: *Journal News* reporter Ernie Palladino got on my nerves, and I got pissed. That's Russ Salzberg of WWOR-TV trying to intervene.

May 1996: I was arrested by the Myrtle Beach Police for trying to buy a hundred dollars' worth of crack cocaine from undercover agents.

Reuters photo/Lisa DeJong

November 1999: In a staredown with my lawyer, Angelo Ferlita, in court. I pleaded no contest to drug charges in St. Petersburg, Florida, after a police informant testified that he sold me fifty dollars' worth of crack cocaine.

August 7, 1999: This was one of the greatest days of my life. T. J. presented me at the Pro Football Hall of Fame, I heard "LT!" chants through the air once again, and my family and friends were by my side. I was the 199th inductee and the final one in the twentieth century. Hey, maybe things didn't turn out too bad after all.

The surgery was the following day. The nurse came in with a needle and I passed out. I hate needles. When they wheeled me into the operating room, I had my big black straw golf hat and aquamarine silk underwear on. When I came to after the surgery, my dick was hanging out and five nurses were standing there gawking at it.

When I got back to my room, I was starving, so I sent my wife and friend Gina out for some smothered pork chops, macaroni and cheese, corn bread, black-eyed peas, and collard greens. I didn't think any of that was going to be on the hospital dinner menu.

Giants co-owner Bob Tisch arranged for me to have a private room, which quickly became filled with flowers and cards from well-wishers. There was a bar across the bed with a morphine drip and I was supposed to press a button whenever the pain became unbearable. Well, I had a violent reaction to the morphine and ripped the bar off the bed and threw it across the room.

I had announced at the beginning of October that I would retire at the end of the season, but now I was telling everyone that I hadn't made a decision yet about whether I had played my last game. Before the injury, I had been feeling like my old self: against the Redskins, I sacked Mark Rypien and forced a fumble, and I had a sack and a forced fumble against the Packers. And I had too much pride to leave the game like that. I wanted to leave the way a warrior should leave. I wanted to be standing at the end of the war.

The Giants wanted me to wear a walking-cast boot, but I told Ronnie, "If you treat this Achilles like a pussy, it's going to heal like a pussy." After a week or two of healing, I started wearing cowboy boots, or golf shoes.

It wasn't long before Dr. Warren brought me into his office and said, "You're going to ruin the surgery and I'm not going to stand for it." I had to do it his way for a couple of weeks before I could go back to the cowboy boots.

When I came out of his office, I told Ronnie, "That sonuvabitch is feisty!"

The nurses told me I was the only person they'd seen who was allowed to walk on a ruptured Achilles at the end of three weeks.

Handley was fired after we'd gone 6–10 in '92, but there was no way George Young was bringing Bill back, so he hired Dan Reeves. I enjoyed playing for Dan. He knew the game of football. Maybe a little too nice to coach in New York.

By this time, I'd already signed my retirement papers. I wanted to take my last tour of the league and get the fuck outta there. It's funny, when I first started playing it was like, "Damn, as soon as the game's over, I can't wait to play the next week." Now I couldn't wait for it to be over.

COREY MILLER

That whole year I remember he was real quiet. He didn't seem as motivated as he was the previous couple of years. I used to have to wake his ass up to go out on the field. I'd have to shake him: "Lawrence, we gotta go on the field!"

I wasn't leaving the game the best player, but I was far from a has-been. No one felt sorry for me. I wasn't LT all the time, but I was LT enough of the time to help us go 11–5 and make the playoffs for the first time since Super Bowl XXV. I could pick my spots like Ali did at the end of his career. You know, rope-a-dope here, rope-a-dope there. Until I ran out of rope. I had six sacks that season, and finished my career with 132.5.

DAN REEVES, Giants head coach

I was proud of him. He would stay for all the meetings, and I had heard that that was something he hadn't done in the past. He knew defenses backward and forward and he was a leader who showed all the young guys what they needed to do.

Certainly that is true, as my young colleague Jessie Armstead would tell you. He became a great defensive player for the Giants (he's with the Redskins now), and was one of our draft choices in 1993. He was an undersized linebacker, but I liked his spunk. One day I told him, "Party at my place. You want to be there." It was time for his rookie initiation. What better way to welcome him to the Giants than a live sex show?

STEVE DeOSSIE

The place was filled with strippers, and LT was acting like he was Oliver Stone, directing the action. "Okay, you stand here, you move this way, you come over here, you step up here." After a while, LT gets the urge for a lap dance, which shouldn't have shocked anyone. Except it quickly turned out to be more than your average lap dance. Armstead sat there the whole time and watched it all with the widest eyes you ever saw.

Another one of the young guys was Michael Strahan, a rookie defensive end who joined us in my final season.

MICHAEL STRAHAN

I was always behind Lawrence [at the Saturday walk-throughs]. And if he was in a good mood, he was out there practicing golf swings, or he was trying to hit a golf ball out of the stadium. And if he wasn't in a good mood, he'd just stand there and stare at you and scare the hell out of you.

He used to come into the meeting rooms and just put his hands behind his head, lay on the floor—I don't know if he was sleeping or not—and every time the coach [defensive coordinator Mike Nolan or defensive line coach Earl Leggett] put in a new blitz or something, he'd always go, "Is that okay with you, Lawrence? Does that seem like it'll work to you?" So Lawrence was like the most respected player I've ever seen in football.

Dan cut me plenty of slack to save me for Sundays. Most of my teammates understood this, even the old-timers like Phil.

PHIL SIMMS

I'd be going to practice, and he'd be getting a massage, and he'd stay inside and read his Bible in the locker room. We were all standing on the practice field one day—I think Bart Oates was with me—and we were having a little chuckle: "Lawrence didn't have to come to practice." I look in the parking lot, and I see a Jaguar come flying through there. It was Lawrence leaving. So much for reading the Bible.

We would laugh. We just kinda appreciated the fact that somebody was beating the system. We all fight for our lives trying to keep our job, and he's leaving practice.

By '93 Phil and I were part of the older generation of Giants. We didn't have a whole lot in common with the kids coming in and it made Phil and me a little closer. I remember we were beating the Saints in a Monday-night game and about to go 11–3.

PHIL SIMMS

Lawrence was sitting on the sidelines. I kinda slapped him on the shoulder and said, "We can win this whole sonuvabitch!" I think it was the first time I actually believed we had a chance to work our way into position where we could do a lot better than our talent.

Well, not exactly. After thirteen years, it all came to an end on a cool January day in Candlestick Park. The 49ers kicked our asses, 44–3, in the NFC Divisional playoff game. Oh, well. It would have been nice to win a third Super Bowl with the Giants, but how could I complain? I had made my mark in the game, and had won two championships. And I knew it was time for me to go. I was thirty-four years old. I had nothing left to give.

Man, was I going to miss this fantasy world I'd lived in. If I fucked up on the street, I could always come back in that stadium and redeem myself on Sundays, and get the fans behind me again. There was no bigger high than running out of that tunnel and onto the field every Sunday at 1 P.M., with seventy thousand Giant fans screaming "LT! LT! LT!" I'd look up into the stands and see a section where all the fans had my number 56 jersey on, and then I'd look over by the thirty-yard line and see a section where *everybody* sitting there had been sitting in those same seats from day one, long before I got to New York even. I used to love standing in the tunnel, waiting to be introduced. The PA announcer would say my name, and I'd go running out there, and the crowd would go crazy. That used to send chills up my back. Used to put some tears in my eyes, too.

I don't want to sound cocky, but I played the game at a different level. I changed the way the game was played. I showed that defense can be played offensively. Let's dictate some shit.

I played with enthusiasm. I don't see anybody out there today who plays the game with more enthusiasm than I did.

When my grandchildren ask me who LT was, I'm going to tell 'em the same thing everybody else says: He was a bad motherfucker. Sometimes it was hard living up to being Superman. There were some games I flat-out shouldn't have played. But I lived for those moments when we were in the huddle and the other team was driving and it was nut-cuttin' time, and Harry Carson or Bill Parcells would look over to me and say, "LT, you have to make a play for us."

PETER KING

His legacy is that he's the most feared defensive player in NFL history. He rose to the occasion better than any player, defensive or offensive, in NFL history. He's the best player I've seen in nineteen years covering the NFL. LT made it fashionable for somebody to put the best athlete of the team, not just a plugger but the fast, speedy guy, at linebacker to go rush the quarterback. He became the prototype for a generation of outside linebackers to follow him. A guy who made it very, very hard for quarterbacks to breathe.

When all the cameras are rollin', and you know the shit's going to happen right *here*—those were the moments I played for, lived for. Some guys don't like that kind of pressure, but that's what separates the good players from the great players. You think Michael Jordan wanted Scottie Pippen shooting the free throws at the end of the game? Hell, no. He wanted to be on that line. I wanted to be on that line.

Now I was on the sideline of the last game of my career. I didn't want it to end like this, but there was nothing I could do to change that score, so I stood there with my arms crossed, tears in my eyes, waiting for the clock to run out.

COREY MILLER

He had a look on his face like he couldn't believe it was over. I don't know that he really wanted it to be over. I remember him crying, tears in his eyes. Kinda in a haze, just kinda out of it. It was a sad day for him, a sad day for the organization, a sad day for his teammates. We all hated that he was gonna be gone.

After the game, I went down to the press room to tell the world what everybody already knew. When Phil Simms finished his interview, he stepped down from the podium and hugged me. I almost lost it. It didn't fully hit me until then that football was over for me. I was a month shy of my thirty-fifth birthday. Here's part of the Q&A from my last press conference as a New York Giant:

Q: *Why is this your last game?*
A: Because I've done everything I can do. I've been to Super Bowls, I've been to playoffs, I've been able to do things in this game that haven't been done before. I've earned the respect of players and people in general around the coun-

try. That's all you want to do when you pick a career, and that's what I've done. I'm happy with the thirteen years I put in, and it's time for me to go.

Q: *Is this the way you wanted it to end?*

A: That's not even a smart question, so I don't think that deserves an answer.

Q: *Who were you looking for when you walked onto the field at the end of the game?*

A: I went to look for the ref because I'd asked him in the third quarter if I could have his yellow flag when the game was over. He's thrown it against me enough, so I thought I would take it from him.

Q: *What are you going to miss about the game?*

A: I'm going to miss just being around the guys because I've been playing with the New York Giants for thirteen years. It's family to me. That has been my world for a lot of years. To change that and to go in a different direction . . . Instead of making that left turn to go down to the locker room, I'll be going up toward the stands. That will be a little bit different. I'll miss the fans.

Q: *[49ers running back] Ricky Watters said you told him [during the game] that he was running well. He said that meant as much to him as anything that has happened to him.*

A: Well, hell, I should've told him he was running like shit.

Q: *Would you like to pursue coaching?*

A: Oh, no, no, no! I might get an asshole like me, so I don't want to deal with that. There's more to life than sweat every day. It's time to move on to other things now.

Q: *What won't you miss about the game?*

A: I won't miss curfew. I missed curfew a couple times . . .

Q: *Are you glad it's over?*

A: Yeah, I am glad it's over.

I didn't know what I wanted to do after football. I thought maybe I'd go into business. For the most part, my future was up in the air. I did have one firm commitment, though. Sometime that week, maybe even that day, I reminded myself, "I'm going to start doing recreational drugs again." I'd been tested by the NFL for so long, and I remember thinking, "Hey, no more pissin' in the bottle." I must have led the daggone league in pissin' in a bottle. Football is a huge thrill. Cocaine gave me something to look forward to. Now there was nothing stopping me. And nothing to keep me from going back to cocaine.

I didn't have to worry anymore about letting down Wellington Mara and my teammates. I'd been thinking about it for weeks, and was so excited that I would go and tell people outright, like Phil and Ronnie Barnes.

PHIL SIMMS

We were alone in the TV room adjacent to the locker room when Lawrence told me he planned on going back to recreational drugs after his last game. He would say some crazy stuff. You just laugh. When he said it, you didn't know if he meant it or was saying it for a laugh.

I'd had a lot of fun when I was on drugs, and I knew that I would need something to replace the thrill of football.

RONNIE BARNES

He told me, "When I stop playing, and when you guys aren't testing me anymore, I'm going to live as hard as I want and take all the drugs I want."

To understand my mind-set back then, I saw the coke as the only bright spot in my future. I realized that for the last couple of years, I had been reeling. I was reading the Bible every day. I was going to church every Sunday. I was coming off a devastating injury, and I wasn't enjoying the game the way I once had. Bill was gone, as were many of the guys I'd gone to war with. I was searching for something to comfort me, something that would tell me everything was going to be all right.

On the personal front, my marriage had collapsed. There are a lot of stories like this, but here are two that are pretty fucked-up. The first happened when I ran into Linda at some club in Winston-Salem, where I was playing in a golf tournament.

LINDA

He was with a girl and I went up to her and said, "I'm Lawrence Taylor's wife; who are you?" I was with my mom and her two sisters.

Later that night, back at the hotel, Lawrence became enraged and began throwing my clothes out the door. He cursed at my mother. Security was summoned. He acted like *he* had caught *me* with a man.

BOB PUTT, general manager of LT's

I had to go to WFAN to conduct some business sometime in 1990, and while I was there, Lawrence was talking to one of the secretaries. He wound up leaving with her. This was not uncommon for Lawrence.

The next morning, I got this emergency phone call to turn on FAN, and Imus is interviewing the girl, and asking her about the date: "Were you soul-kissing?" and all that crap. Lawrence was married, and this interview is taking place on his kid's birthday. The party was gonna be at his restaurant that night. I went to the restaurant that afternoon, and Lawrence always came in the back door and came up to my office upstairs.

I said, "I gotta tell you something," and it was one of the few times I've seen him lose his temper. He used to drink these shaker glasses full of fruit punch. He threw the glass across the room and it crashed on the wall in my office. He was sitting opposite my desk.

He stood over my desk and said, "You get me [WFAN general manager] Joel Hollander on the phone NOW!" I got Joel on the phone and Joel basically said he didn't really have any control over Imus in this case. LT told Hollander, "You have to get your boy under control."

Needless to say, it wasn't a pleasant evening. I remember Linda putting on a good front at the party but being pretty angry at him.

Let's just say I was a better football player than I was a husband. My buddy Paul Davis and I used to go to this bar that *opened* at two in the morning. When all the bars in New Jersey closed, we'd go to Jimmy Day's. Linda didn't want me going, of course, so I would tell Paul, who was living with us, "Take the car to the end of the street and I'll sneak out through the garage and meet you there." Linda used to think I was downstairs sleeping in the basement.

Linda and I used to throw some mean New Year's Eve parties. We had three-quarters of the team over at our house some years. We'd hire entertainers, bands, even a magician Bill Cosby introduced me to. He would do some great magic tricks. My favorite was the one where he put me in this specially made box and then locked me up with handcuffs. When he put those handcuffs on me, I said something like, "I've been here before." That broke everyone up. Those magic days disappeared in a hurry, though.

LINDA

The worst New Year's came on a Cruise to Nowhere one year. I never should have gone. We were already mad at each other. I had gone to Cape Cod with my girlfriend and it got real foggy, so we didn't want to drive back. He started accusing me of cheating on him. We weren't sitting beside each other. He had invited a friend; supposedly it was another couple. I got the feeling this particular girl liked him. I'd been drinking champagne with some of the other players' wives and got up from the table, and when I returned I saw her hand was on his leg; I just lost it. We ended up in the bathroom arguing, and I hit him. I was a little over the edge, I must say. He took me in the bathroom, trying not to cause a scene. I don't remember where I hit him, but I was just swinging! I was calling him all kinds of names. We ended up going home.

Linda filed for divorce in 1989. She had been my college sweetheart, and I was crushed when we split, even though I had put her through hell. One of the worst moments for my family and me was at Paul Davis's wedding on August 31, 1991. I was his best man. The moving men were coming to the house that day, but my daughters were flower girls, and my son T.J. was an usher, so we had to go through with the wedding.

LINDA

There were two sides to Lawrence; there might have been three. To his mother, he was Lonnie. The Lawrence Taylor side, the one I fell in love with, was sweet and caring. Then there was the LT side that New York made. LT was a maniac. There's no other word for it. I used to say to him, "I'm not a fan of yours. I'm your wife."

At first, I stayed with him as long as I did for my kids. And then, you just always have hope. You knew he was try-

ing, and then to turn your back on him would have set him back. Every time I would threaten to leave, he would straighten up for about a month, and he would start all over again.

Finally, though, he was, for me, starting to be more verbally abusive to the kids. I just knew they couldn't continue to live like that. I knew I had to leave.

BOBBY CUPO

Linda had enough of the infidelity. She had enough of Lawrence Taylor. She wanted to be Linda Cooley. She didn't want to be Mrs. Lawrence Taylor. She wanted her own life. She wanted her independence.

After dinner, Linda and I got up for one last dance. She started crying, and then I started crying, and pretty soon it seemed like everyone in the room was crying along with us.

And then Linda took the kids and was gone. They were moving back to Charlotte the next day. I went back to my table and sat there in silence. We eventually reconciled, but in 1992, she filed again, this time for good. Actually, for bad. She was awarded custody of the children when the divorce became official in 1996.

LINDA

I think the judge for our divorce was an LT fan. At the end of the trial, he asked for Lawrence's autograph.

Our separation really got me down. I was angry at myself, angry at the world, and this just added to the misery I was feeling. Lately, even when I was having fun and raising hell, even when everyone was calling me Superman, I wasn't truly happy. Maybe for three hours on Sundays I was happy, but once I took that number 56 off, it was a different story.

Even strangers could see the conflict raging inside me. Religious people would come up to me and say, "I want to talk to you. You have demons inside you." Even though I was—as far as they knew—sitting on top of the world, they could see that there was a demon inside me fighting to get out. Now he was about to come out.

I mostly slept on the plane ride home from San Francisco. The next day, I was diving into drugs like Greg Louganis diving into a pool.

CHAPTER ELEVEN

One of the few bright spots in my so-called Life After Football was the night the Giants retired my jersey on October 10, 1994, a *Monday Night Football* game against the Vikings. I stood in the middle of my old field of dreams and looked out at those seventy-five thousand people and said this:

"You know, I should be nervous, but I'm not, because I'm in my house. This is one of the proudest moments I've ever had in Giants Stadium." I thanked Wellington Mara "for always being there for me like a father" and I thanked Bob Tisch for "all his wisdom he showed me." I thanked Bill Parcells, then I spoke directly to the fans again: "This is about you and me. Giant fans. Because you've always been there no matter what was said, no matter what was written, no matter what was going on in my personal life. We've always been in this together. Without you guys here, there would have been a Lawrence Taylor, but there wouldn't have been an LT. Thank you very much."

Pretty good speech, huh? I have a confession. A couple of hours before that ceremony, I called Beasley Reece, who was driving down from Connecticut to be a part of it, and I asked him to write my speech. He wrote it on a McDonald's napkin he found in his glove compartment. I gave it the once-over in the tunnel, ad-libbed the beginning of it, and, I must say, recited the speech as if I had written it myself. When the lights go on, I can perform.

Hell, I even had to perform when they retired Phil Simms's jersey the following year. Out of the blue he said, "I've always wanted to throw a pass to the greatest Giant of all time. Lawrence, go deep. Let me throw one more pass in Giants Stadium." I was terrified I would drop it. Of course, I didn't.

Dan invited me back to speak to give a pep talk to his reeling team before a Houston game. I don't remember everything I said, but I do remember telling them this before the kickoff: "You guys are so bad your bitches don't even respect you!"

DAN REEVES

He came in and gave a talk that was probably the best pep talk I've ever heard. The passion he played the game with really came out, how prideful he was being a Giant, how much it meant to him.

Dan must have thought I was a good-luck charm, and he invited me to give another talk to the team early in the '95 season. Afterward, Ernie Palladino of the *Journal News*

wanted to do an interview about what I had said to the team. I said to Ernie and the press, "Guys, this ain't about me. It's about the team on the field. I ain't got nothing to say to you guys." Palladino got pissed off and started following me. And when he said something like, "C'mon, you don't have to do this anymore, you're not an athlete, you don't have to play these games anymore," I said, "That's right, I'm not an athlete, that's why I don't have to talk to you guys anymore."

Then Palladino had the balls to say, "Same bullshit, huh Lawrence?" And I told him, "Watch it, you." And then he says, "Ah, fuck you." He started walking off the field and he turned around and I started screaming, "You wanna fuck with me? You wanna fuck with me?" I started to charge him, twenty yards maybe, and Palladino stuck a finger in my face and said, "You're wrong. You're wrong." I grabbed him around the neck for a second and shoved him back and said, "Get away from me, you dilly-silly bitch!" A couple of media guys pulled him—five-six, one seventy, one eighty—and Vinny DiTrani of the *Bergen Record* stood in front of me. I explained to him, "He cursed me out. That's not necessary, Vinny."

Pat Hanlon, the Giants public relations director, quickly convinced me in the equipment room that it would be a good idea to do a little damage control so the papers wouldn't read so ugly, so I offered Palladino my All-Madden jacket, which I was picking up that day. I told him, "You deserve this, 'cause you're the only guy I know who's crazier than me!"

It was an embarrassing scene, pretty emblematic of all the other shit that was going on in my life.

The drugs were a part of it, naturally, but that was just the beginning.

GEORGE MARTIN

I didn't realize the depths of his problem until Linda called me one day and said, "I want you to come with me up to the house. Lawrence needs us."

We went in the side door, and when Lawrence saw us he went ballistic, screaming and cursing. I backed up a few steps, but Linda stood there, fearless. I said, "Listen, Lawrence, the only reason we're here is we love you. We want to talk to you."

Finally, he said, "If you MFs aren't going to leave, I'll leave." He went down to the garage. Now Lawrence is in the car, with the engine going. I'm standing by the driver's door and he's still ranting and raving. I tell him, "I'm not going to move." I wasn't letting him leave. Thank God he blinked.

He finally came back upstairs, and we sat down and talked. Well, he talked; we listened. He told me how drugs had taken him through the doors of hell.

In addition to my drug problem, and my marital problems, I was getting smacked around like a punk in the business world. As easy as sacking a quarterback had been for me, that's how difficult it was for me to make it happen as an entrepreneur. Some investors and I had started a company called All Pro; we were going to sell a sports drink, but we

put that on the back burner when we got the opportunity to do virtual reality. That was a much easier sell to investors— we raised over $5 million for the company. The brokers took the company public in 1993.

That didn't last long. Hanover Sterling was our underwriter; they got closed down by the SEC for strong-arming people to invest. Apparently, they resold stock at inflated prices without reporting it. When they got closed down, the companies under them got hurt, which meant that I got hurt. Bad. And so did some of my friends. (I wouldn't let anybody put their money into anything unless my money was in there.) When the company went public, I was worth $11 million on paper. When it collapsed in 1995, the company was worth practically nothing, and I lost $3 million. I felt even worse that George Martin, Paul Davis, and my mom took a bath, too.

Then there was my restaurant, LT's. I knew a guy who ran a successful restaurant/bar we all used to go to, so I opened up a place with him. As I said, I was excited about having a place of my own, and it seemed like a great idea at the time. How was I supposed to know he wasn't reputable? The place was always jumping, and he made a lot of money at LT's, but paid no bills. In summer of 1992, LT's was put into receivership and liquidated. I reopened it a few months later after making a new deal with the landlord, but within a year the landlord was issuing default notices, and I had to shut down the place for good.

The Lawrence Taylor Golf & Marina Center was another failure. Never heard of it? Well, I'd be surprised if you did, because it turned into a double bogey in a hurry. Still, I did get a TNT football gig in '94. That was fun. For a while. I was supposed to be spontaneous as an analyst, but I may have been a little too "spontaneous." You see, I can tell you technical things about football, but I don't watch enough games to know all the players. They switched to me on the field one time at the half and Aeneas—pronounced "Uh-KNEE-is"—Williams had done something special for the Cardinals, so I said, "Anus Williams had a big first half," or something like that. I reckon a few jaws dropped across America when they heard that.

I got a lot of heat for wrestling Bam Bam Bigelow in *Wrestlemania XI* in April 1995, but do you think the hypocrites who dogged me for that would turn down $1 million for a little more than eleven minutes' work? Also, I seem to remember Muhammad Ali pocketing a bundle for an exhibition against some Japanese wrestler.

The press conference to announce the match was at the Hard Rock Café. It was a wild scene. Bam Bam, who grew up in Secaucus and was a Giants fan, was there and I called him a big ol' Easter egg and told the press, "I'm going out there like a bunch of crazed dogs." Then we got into this intense stare-down, and I surprised Bam Bam when I broke the tension by kissing him on the cheek.

CARL WHITE, FOX-TV reporter

Stuttering John from the *Howard Stern Show* opened the questioning by asking, "How are you celebrating Black His-

tory Month?" LT didn't hesitate. "Beating up on white guys," he said.

Someone asked, "Would you like to see drugs legalized?" and LT shot back: "Aren't they already?"

Then I asked him, "Has retirement gotten so boring for you that you would stoop to *this*?"

"Stoop?" LT fired back. "You stooped to going on FOX, didn't you?"

It was great. He acted pissed off, but he really wasn't.

The match was cool. The fans at the sold-out Civic Center made me feel like I was in Giants Stadium, and after a couple of forearm smashes and a reverse suplex, that four-hundred-pound bad boy was history!

SCOTT "BAM BAM" BIGELOW

LT was THE MAN. You weren't gonna win if you didn't have LT on the field. He was my hero. I had trouble getting him to train for the match, though. I think I got him twice for an hour each time to show him what we're gonna do in the match. More or less choreograph it. So I was worried that LT hadn't prepared enough, so I warned him that I'd end the match quickly to save us any embarrassment. "If you screw up," I told him, "I'm gonna pin you, and there's not a damn thing you can do about it."

The game plan had LT winning the match, but I went over to Vince McMahon to warn him, too. But he rose to the occasion. Millions and millions of dollars were being spent there. The whole thing was riding on our match. There was a lot of pressure on LT. He did every move we choreographed to a T. He just pulled it off big time.

The only problem was that LT was punching me pretty hard every time—he wasn't used to holding back like we do. Anyway, after about twelve minutes, LT went for the kill with a Power Bomb and pinned me. We knew LT had practiced the move on lighter men. We were hoping in the match, if the situation came up, he was gonna be able to do that with me.

He did it but he was spent. Some of the other football players in the house, including Reggie White, were supposed to lift LT up and carry him around in a victory celebration. But LT was breathing heavily, and his body was limp. They had to put him down and he just flopped and laid down in the ring.

I had the privilege of LT telling me I was one of the best athletes he ever met, and he gave me a gift, too: his Giant rookie helmet.

I was getting nothing but shit from the papers during this period, but all those people tearing me a new asshole never walked in my shoes. They didn't know that I had some bills to pay. There was the $50,000 a month alimony and child support payments to Linda for our three children; the child support payments to my oldest daughter, Whitney, from an ex-girlfriend; the $2,900 a month to the mothers of two children out of wedlock; as well as the Atlantic City casinos, and $1.1 million to the IRS for what I thought was a tax shelter

investment in horses. It's a wonder I didn't have to file for bankruptcy until 1998.

With all these bills piling up, I even thought about playing again. With free agency, it was a whole new ball game out there. I would watch games on TV and know that I could suit up and still play just as good or better than a lot of players. For a couple months, I worked out in Mahwah, lifting weights, running the street in the cold. I actually felt quicker. Parcells was in New England by now, and Belichick was still in Cleveland, but I wasn't thinking of a cold-weather team. If I was going to do it, it was going to be in Florida somewhere. I remember sitting around during a Taco Bell commercial taping and it came up.

BOBBY CUPO

We were at the Westchester Country Club with Phil Simms, Bruce Smith, Howie Long, and Chris Berman. The payment for appearing in the commercial was a hundred thousand dollars. They arrived at 6 A.M., and Taylor, Simms, and I started playing cards to pass the time. Hours passed and Taylor was growing restless. At one point, he said, "Jesus Christ!"

Long was annoyed. "Shut the fuck up. We're stealing money!" Taylor started thinking about it for a second and shut right up.

Later on, Taylor volunteered that he was planning a comeback.

"You aren't coming back," Simms said.

"You wanta make a bet?" Taylor asked.

"I'll bet you one thousand bucks you won't make the starting roster," Simms said.

"Let's make it five thousand," Taylor said.

"I think one thousand is a reasonable bet," Simms said. Just at that moment, Long walked back into the room. He turned to Taylor and said: "For crissakes. You were the best defensive player ever to put on a uniform. Let it go. It's over."

Lawrence didn't say anything. The bet was never made.

Well, so much for support from the guys. But, really, trying to get into shape was more than I was willing to deal with. And the thought of going back to training camp and all that stuff? No thanks. I would even do modest appearances to help with the bills.

SANDRA McNEIL

My husband Stephen was turning forty on July 4, 1996. More than a year earlier, I began planning a special surprise birthday: Stephen, a die-hard Giants and LT fan, would meet number 56 on a cruise around the Statue of Liberty. I had contacted Bobby Cupo, LT's business manager at the time, and sent in a $10,000 deposit. I was supposed to give LT the remaining $15,000 on the Celebrity Cruise Lines boat. I'd been saving money from my job as an X-ray technician for the longest time.

There were about forty of the McNeils' friends and fam-

ily on the boat. Stephen didn't notice LT right away. He was flabbergasted when he did.

"Ohmigod! I can't believe it's you!" he said to LT. During the cutting of the cake, LT presented him with a 56 jersey with his signature on it. Then I gave him a Giants helmet signed by the Super Bowl XXI Giants.

Now it was time for me to give LT the check.

"No," LT said, "you guys are great people. I spoke to your friends about you. Put it toward your daughter's education."

"I can't do that," I told him.

"No way I'm walking out of here with that," LT said. And he didn't. Everybody has their ups and downs, but he has a great heart, and he's an honest person.

Of course, a lot of my money went to drugs. I still thought I could handle the drugs. Sometimes I would tell myself, "Oh shit, I have to stop," but the remorse only lasted for a little while. As soon as my head was clear, I'd say to myself, "Hey, it wasn't that bad. I can still go out and hang."

But it *was* bad. I had a teenage girlfriend from the Bahamas named Sadie. She was eighteen when I started dating her, but she was mature for her age. She had a good personality, and a beautiful smile. She was very intelligent, and a loving person. She was a good companion, but at that point in my life, I wasn't ready for Sadie. The problem wasn't her. It was me. I was no longer LT. I was Lawrence Taylor. And Lawrence Taylor was having a hard time adjusting to Life After LT. Sadie was really getting pissed off at me by this point. I'd say I was going out to get some milk and I would be gone for three days. (Hey, it's hard to find the right kind of milk.) I'd be in a hotel room with a bunch of freaks I had met at a go-go bar, and I didn't want to leave.

I would try the Visine to clear my eyes, but she could always smell it on me, and of course it hurt her. And sometimes she'd act like she didn't know. Of course they know. And the lies I would tell, like "Hey, I'm caught in traffic." Or, "I was over at another hotel with some other people." She'd come to the room knocking on the door, and I'd call the front desk people and tell them, "Don't let her know I'm here. Just come get her and tell her I'm gone." It wasn't because I was ashamed—I wasn't finished! If she stayed with me at the hotel, I would get another room I could get high in, in somebody else's name, of course, and then shower up and go back into the room and go to bed. I learned every trick in the book.

When I would go on one of my cocaine binges, I could be on the seventeenth floor of a hotel, but I'd close the blinds and peer out the windows because I was afraid that people were watching me use. I had become so paranoid that I would crawl on the floor so that nobody could see my shadow on the blinds.

BOBBY CUPO

He used to go out on his binges and I couldn't find him, which was a problem when I was trying to make deals for him. One time, we had an opening offer of $130,000 for a

TV show. I always conferred with Taylor, but now I couldn't find him. Then I thought of a new strategy. I'd give the impression that Taylor was holding out for a better deal. I told the guy, "You gotta sweeten the pot."

I got him another $50,000, needless to say.

When I got home from one of those three-day crack fests, my good friend Gary Gaglioti was there, waiting for me. He told me that he had called Charlie Stucky. Gary had told Charlie that I was having some difficulties and that Charlie needed to come talk with me. I was so mad at Gary that I said, "Man, don't even talk to me again."

But Gary kept coming over to my house, for something like ten days straight. I wouldn't even open the door for him, but finally, I did, and we got into an argument about my drug abuse. I finally said to him, "What, are *you* going to kick my ass?"

Gary, who's short and stocky, said, "I'm going to give it a college try."

Charlie began to call me and say, "Why don't you come see me?" But I always found excuses for putting him off. I was in denial. I didn't think I had a problem. But Sadie kept saying I had to do something, and I had some contractual obligations coming up, so I decided that I needed to do something. The cocaine made me irresponsible. I would make appointments and forget them, and stand people up. It was hurting business.

I checked into Honesty House as an inpatient on December 5, 1995. A couple of days later, I told my counselor, Bill

Schoonover, that an ominous pattern had developed in my life. I told him I would actually plan the times of my cocaine use, and schedule any personal activities around it. That worked for a while . . . and then I'd become dependent on the drug and couldn't stop.

Unlike everyone else staying at Honesty House, I had my own room. I had made all these demands. No roommate. I want a TV in my room, with cable. A cell phone. These are all things you aren't supposed to have, but Charlie knew that giving them to me was the only way he was going to be able to keep me there.

A typical day at Honesty House is breakfast at a quarter to eight, then classes from nine-thirty until ten-thirty, unless Charlie's leading the sessions—then they might last until eleven, because he's long-winded. Lunch at twelve, then another class from one-thirty to two-thirty. Then we'd have a rap session from three to four, dinner at five-thirty, another meeting at seven-thirty that lasts an hour, and then lights-out at eleven.

Charlie didn't know it, but when I wasn't in meetings, I was banging everything in that bad boy. Just killing every-thing. Bad habits die hard, man.

Some funny shit goes on in rehab. You had this one scary guy, skinny with black hair—he thought he was a fucking vampire. In fact, he had a big old plug out of his arm where he had gnawed himself. And one of my best friends there looked like a frog, so we used to kid around and call him "The Frog." Some serious shit goes on, too. You hear about heroin, but I had never seen the withdrawal those addicts suffer. Ooooh, that's an ugly sight to see when somebody's trying to kick heroin. Real ugly.

Everyone took notes at the meetings. I didn't. There would be meetings outside Honesty House at *this place* on Monday and *that place* on Wednesday and *this other place* on Friday and *that other place* on Saturday morning. Groups from different houses would get together, but I would never go. I didn't want to be mixing with strangers. I didn't want other people to know where I was. Or why.

The thing I hated most was standing up in front of a group and saying, "My name is Lawrence Taylor and I'm an addict." We had to do that every day. In our rap sessions, a guy would tell his story—how he got high, what he did, how much stuff he was doing in his life—and I would say to myself, "This motherfucker is fucked-up! I haven't done half the shit these people have done. What the hell am I doing here? When I get that bad, *then* I need to be here." I never told my story in group sessions.

In other words, I was bullshitting everybody. My first stay at Honesty House wasn't like rehab. It was more like just detox. I didn't go in to learn anything. I just went in to sober up. It was a little vacation. Every time I would give Charlie my reasons for leaving, he would say, "If bullshit was music, you'd sound like a brass band." I stayed for fourteen days.

When I was saying my good-byes, Charlie said, "Make me a deal—if you mess up again, you come for the whole pro-gram, which is twenty-eight days." I said, "Fine, Charlie, fine." I didn't think I was coming back. He knew I'd be back.

Bill and Charlie set up a support network for me—a

psychiatrist and a clinician in the NFL substance abuse program—and an intensive outpatient aftercare program.

A week later, I went to the Bahamas with Sadie on the twenty-sixth. I got high that night.

Sadie was visiting her mother there, so I told her, "You stay with your mom tonight, I'm going to stay at the hotel and gamble." I gambled all right. With my life.

A half hour after I dropped Sadie off, I had some coke in my hands. You see, I'd been getting shit from the same people in the Bahamas for so long that I didn't even have to leave my hotel room. They'd bring it to me. Now, that's what I call room service.

In a matter of days, I was smoking all the time. I went on a binge that continued when we got back to New Jersey. Hell, that binge lasted three or four months. I had other distractions as well. The IRS was on my ass for tax evasion stuff connected to LT's.

Any excuse to get out of the house was good enough for me at that point. I had a golf tournament in Myrtle Beach, so I jumped on a plane and got there a few days early. I played golf all day, then went back to my room. I was pretending that I was going to be a good little boy, but I was in my room, alone, watching television, bored as hell. After a while, I thought to myself, "There are fine women all over town, and I'm sitting by myself watching television? Hell, no. Let's have some fun."

I'd been coming to Myrtle Beach to play golf for years, and had been buying crack there for years, so I went looking for a guy who used to sell me shit. One thing about a drug user—he remembers every spot where he bought. All across

the country. He remembers every fuckin' spot. Sure enough, I found this guy's house, but he didn't sell me anything that night. He told me to come back the next day.

The next morning, I tee off at 7:30 and play thirty-six holes. There's a pairings party for the tournament and a sports memorabilia benefit auction at 7 P.M., so I shower and hustle over to the guy's house and say, "Got anything for me?" He had something for me. He had $100 of fake crack. He had been busted the night before, and he tried to make a deal with the cops by selling me out.

As I look back on it now, I should have realized I was being set up—there was this little old lady across the street, sweet thing, and guys riding bikes up and down the street . . . Guess what? Everybody on that block was a cop. The cops set up a sting operation.

I give the guy $100 for his "crack," and next thing I know, there are cars coming at me from every direction, and cops with guns spilling out of them. "Hit the ground!" they yelled. Even the old lady pulled a gun on me. They slammed me down on the pavement. I said, "Oh, fuck." The first thing I thought of was what the headline in tomorrow's paper was going to be: LT BUSTED!

They took me to the police station, and I could hear them calling the TV stations. "We got him!" I was charged with intent to purchase. I must say, however, that they were perfect gentlemen at the police station. I got fingerprinted—when I wasn't signing autographs—but they didn't make me go through all the standard bullshit, and before long, I was in a taxi heading back to my hotel.

When I got back to my room, I realized that I still had enough time to make it to the pairings party, so I jumped in the shower, got dressed, and went on down.

I start shaking hands and acting as if nothing had happened. Of course, it's the last place I wanted to be, but I had given my word that I would be there. Steve DeOssie and Matt Bahr were there; I told DeOssie that some shit was coming down, but he thought I was talking about some paternity suit.

The first reporter who got ahold of me was Nick Nicholas, who was the golf writer at the *Myrtle Beach Sun News* back then.

NICK NICHOLAS

I went to the Yachtsman Hotel and called Matt Bahr from the hotel lobby to get a reaction. It was about 10:40 P.M. local time. I think I woke him up. He gave me a quote or two. By that time the guy behind the desk said, "Are you looking for Mr. Taylor?" I said, "Yeah." He said, "Well, he's right behind you." He had just come in with a bag of food; I guess he'd been to a fast-food restaurant.

I asked him point-blank: "I understand you've been arrested for buying cocaine," and he denied it. LT waited in the lobby and he was a little startled when I was on the phone with my editor. He waited for me to come back over there and said, "Does the press already know about this?" He goes, "Okay, let me talk to you."

We went outside to the side of the hotel and sat on the

grass by the sidewalk. It was a beautiful night. You could see the ocean. I asked LT if I could turn on my tape recorder. LT, his arms on his knees, said no.

He was wearing sunglasses, but they couldn't hide his pain. "My life is in the shitter," he said. He even said, "Maybe I ought to kill myself." I was startled and told him, "That's the last thing you ought to be thinking about."

Sometime after that, LT let me turn on the tape recorder. He confirmed the sting and talked about how he had hurt his family. He was just in shock. I'd never met the guy. The only time I'd ever seen him was drilling quarterbacks.

LT spoke very quietly. After the fifteen-minute interview ended, I walked LT back to the lobby. Then I went back to the office to give the quotes to reporter Jeannine F. Hunter.

Now I knew the shit was going to hit the fan. I was desperate for help and called Tommy Brittain, a local attorney who I played with in the charity golf tournament the day before. I needed someone on my side. I had Tommy pulled out of a movie theater, where he was out with his family.

TOMMY BRITTAIN

When I got there, there was a bunch of press people outside down below. My problem is, in this little area of the world, I'm kind of a known quantity myself. Several of them knew me and knew the kind of things I do. I was immediately bombarded with questions. I could only offer "no comments" and shrugs as I made my way to the elevator. The desk clerk was looking for me, and he said LT was staying in the penthouse.

I knocked on the door. LT's girlfriend asked, "Can I help you?" I could hear LT yell out, "Is that Tommy Brittain?" and I said, "This is me." LT said, "Let him in, let him in."

I was shocked at what I saw. He was distraught, he was hugging a pillow, laying up on the couch, knees up under him, crying.

"You gotta help me, man. You gotta help me, man. You gotta help me."

LT's girlfriend was trying to calm him down. I put on a brave front. "I can skin this cat," I told him. "You just relax. It's gonna be okay. There's not gonna be a problem with this."

By the next morning a horde of reporters were camped out at the hotel. I couldn't even leave my room. Even the airport was covered. I freaked out. I was so distraught that I flew Charlie down from New Jersey because I needed someone to tell me everything was going to be all right.

I told Charlie I didn't know why I had gone out looking for drugs, and how sorry I was for fucking up.

I left the hotel that night—down the fire escape and out the back. A friend flew me home in his private jet.

The worst part about this arrest was what Linda and our kids had to go through. I'm a celebrity, and it was open season.

LINDA

I just started crying. I had to tell my kids before it hit the news. I think I woke them up that night. They were sad, and they cried. They didn't want to go to school, but I emphasized to them that you can't run away from it.

T.J.

It was hell. I hated being around people at those times. I tried to avoid people as much as I could. People could be nosy; people could be harsh; and sometimes I didn't want to go to school, but I had to do it. I knew who my friends were. I only hung out with a select few.

WHITNEY TAYLOR DAVIS

When I was young, I wrote my father a letter. My father wasn't the easiest person to talk to during those times. You'd try not to piss him off. I just wanted to reach out to him. My issues with him were, "Where are you?" basically. "Why haven't I heard from you?" There was a lot of space between us and I didn't understand why. I can't say he was the perfect father and has always been there for me every time I needed him, but I didn't begrudge him for anything that happened. I told him I was praying for him, and that it scared me what he was doing. I wanted him to be there when everybody graduated high school and when everybody got married.

It kills me to know that my kids suffered as a result of my bullshit. In my own mind, I tried to put a positive spin on it. I had always been up-front with my kids about the nightmare I was going through with drugs. Sometimes I even think that I'm *glad* I went through that hell because they won't have to go through it. They lived it through me.

The day after I got back to Jersey, Charlie picked me up and took me back to Honesty House. I broke down in his car and cried. I didn't want to go back to rehab, but I knew I needed to go. This was no longer a game. I'd been arrested. This was real-life shit. It was August 30, 1996. When I got to Honesty House, Bill came upstairs to my room and sat on the edge of my bed.

BILL SCHOONOVER, LT's counselor at Honesty House

I saw a broken man that day. He said, "I'm done. This is it. I can't take this anymore."

I said, "Engage in prayer with me." And we put our hands in each other's hands and we just sat together as tears fell down his face.

I went through withdrawal over the weekend, and because somebody had forgotten to leave written instructions for the medical department, they couldn't give me any medication to help me with my anxiety until Monday. I was feeling *extremely* depressed.

On Monday morning I sat in my room feeling stupid and embarrassed. The only good news was that my attorney had made a deal with the judge in South Carolina: the arrest would be wiped away from my record if I complied with the terms of the pretrial intervention. In other words, if I completed the program set up by Honesty House.

I sat down with Bill that day and asked him to give me the tools to beat cocaine. I told him I could handle the drug for about ninety days, and then all hell would break loose. I told him that since my retirement, I had no motivation to stay clean. I was bored, so why not use? I told him how I avoided responsibility. How I let people handle everything for me. I told him that I had no problem-solving skills, and that I had a hard time coping with uncomfortable situations.

For the first seven days, all I did was go to the meetings, and play basketball. I became the house's sports director. I organized tournaments. If someone didn't wake up on time, I'd be pissed, and I'd go around knocking on doors. I'd get all the other patients out for calisthenics in the morning. I got my golf clubs and would hit balls into the woods. We were playing Ping-Pong, cards, horseshoes every night. I tried to make it seem like a country club. Instead of being there to get help, I was trying to make it a camp experience.

I was working on my body, but my head was still messed up. My attitude wasn't very good about the program. Once again, I wasn't there because I wanted to be there; I was there because someone said I had to be there. After two weeks, though, I started making progress. I started understanding the program. I started to understand what drugs were about, how they affected my body, why I had the cravings, why I couldn't stop them.

By the third week, it hit me that I truly wanted to be clean. I don't know why. Even more important, I also started thinking, "Hey, I *can* get clean!" I started taking notes in meetings. I started asking other people in the house what tools they used to beat the Enemy.

The outside world was still kicking my ass, of course. On September 10, I got a call from an opportunistic attorney handling a paternity suit against me. On top of that, my day in divorce court with Linda was a week away. But I didn't freak out. I was surprised that I was able to handle things as well as I did.

The next day my attorney came by to inform me that a warrant had been issued for my arrest. Nobody had told the court where I was. Now I freaked a little bit. I became agitated, and a sense of resignation came over me. But I pushed on, continued to work the program. On the sixteenth, I was discharged from Honesty House.

A lot of people think that as soon as you become clean, you're going to walk outside and—hey—"It's a brand new daaaaay!" No. Because now you have to face the bullshit you had done. There is still a price to be paid. One thing I still had to learn was that you don't become an addict in one day, and you sure as hell don't get straight in one day.

I had called my kids from Honesty House when I checked in there and apologized to them. When I got out, they came up to New Jersey to stay with me for a week. We would talk.

They were very attentive; I could tell they were taking note of what I was saying. They asked a few questions, told me they loved me, and we went on from there.

WHITNEY TAYLOR DAVIS

We [Linda and T.J. and Paula and Tanisha] got him on a speakerphone. We told him we loved him, and things like, "What are you doing? We don't want to see you like this. You gotta stop what you're doing. You can't do this anymore! We want you here alive!"

He said he loved us, too. That's all he could say. I don't think he really wanted to hear it, but at the same time, he realized it was important to us that he did listen.

I also had a heart-to-heart with T.J.

T.J.

Paul Davis drove my father to pick me up at George Martin's house, and we sat in the backseat and talked for three hours. We had no destination, we just drove around. He looked like he had been up for the last couple of days. He was crying and apologizing. He said he was going to change his life around. He was just talking about life; you make wrong decisions sometimes even though you know they're wrong. A lot of times I felt the reasons why he kept relapsing was because me and my sisters weren't around. I put my arm around him and told him everything would be okay.

I thought I was on the road to recovery. I was more relaxed, and able to deal with things more positively. I was no longer obsessing about using. As part of my court deal, Honesty House set up a personal appearance for me with the athletic department at Rutgers. Here's what I told that gym full of students and teachers:

"Addiction cost me everything. It cost me my family, it cost me my name. I was the biggest, baddest, toughest SOB you could ever meet. Nobody, and nothing, could beat me, but cocaine did."

I also spoke at a drug and alcohol prevention program at William Paterson College. I told them, "When you get down to it, you can't save your face and your ass at the same time."

On October 26, 1996, Bill presented me with a ninety-day token, a bronze medallion the size of a quarter. It signified that I had been sober for ninety days. I was proud.

Bill told me, "This is a big breakthrough for you. You're in new waters. You're on the other side of the Wall."

"Yup, you're right," I said.

I stayed clean for about a year.

CHAPTER TWELVE

I'd been lucky—Sadie had stuck with me through my rehab, and we were still living together. But still, I felt a big cloud of bad luck hanging over me, and while there were times I thought I was ready to deal with the straight world, there were lots of other times I wasn't. And I took that out on Sadie. I was tired of being responsible for her happiness. I didn't want to be in charge of *anybody's* happiness except my own. I was, of course, feeling sorry for myself.

So Sadie and I started falling out, arguing constantly. What we argued about is not important. It could be about two birds sitting in a nest. During my druggie days, my attitude toward her was, "Hey, whatever way you want to do it is fine by me," because I'd do anything to keep her happy . . . and to keep her off my back about the drugs. Now, though, I didn't have that noose around my neck, and I wanted to do what made *me* happy.

Things weren't working out. I'm sober, but it's what the counselors call a drunk sober. I wasn't getting high, but I was still in that depressed state, a dry-alcoholic state. I still had everyday problems. Hey, I led the league in everyday problems. I was involved in five different court cases during this period, and I wasn't making much happen in the business world. I had been stabbed in the back so many times by "partners" that it was hard for me to build trust again.

I sent Sadie home. Six weeks later, the Enemy struck again.

It's 1998 now. My routine was: Play golf all day. Come home, eat, and watch the Sci-fi Channel until I fall asleep. I'm doing this every day. Me, myself, and sci-fi. I said to myself, "This is what I got sober for?"

I was sliding toward oblivion.

Around this time, the cops in my town must have gotten together, taken a vote, and decided to start messing with me. It might have been fun for them, but it was no fun for me.

Early one morning I was driving my kids to the airport when I got pulled over. I was driving with a suspended license, so the cop put handcuffs on me, shoved me into the back of his car, and took me to the station. In front of my kids! For a suspended license! I posted a bond and got out right away.

That night, there was a big storm in my area. Lightning hit a tree, which fell over, and knocked out all the power on my street. I didn't feel like sitting in the dark all night, so I drove to the hotel down the road to check in. The cop who had arrested me that morning was sitting in the parking lot. He arrested me. Again.

This was one of the many times I said to myself, "Must be

nice to be rich and white in America!" I remember the night Gary Gaglioti was pulled over for speeding at three in the morning. We were on our way home from a long day—and evening—at the Twin Brook Golf Club.

"Officer," Gary said, "you might as well take out your gun and just shoot me now. I don't have my license, I don't have my registration, I don't have my insurance cards, I don't have nothing."

The cop didn't shoot him. Didn't even give him a ticket. It turns out the owner of Twin Brook let some of the local cops play for free on weekdays, so this guy says, "No problem, Mr. Gaglioti," and lets us go.

As we're pulling away, I turn to Gary, shake my head, and say, "White America!"

He says, "What would have happened to you in that situation?"

I said, "I woulda been on the hood of the car!"

I even got arrested for having dogs. I had two rottweiler puppies. One was named Kick and the other was named Ass. (What else was I going to call them? Filthy and McNasty?) They were house dogs, but they were smart, and they were good at getting out. Out of my house, and out of my yard.

I got forty-one summonses for them running loose. It seemed like I was in court every other day. Pretty soon, the judge is tired of seeing me, and I'm tired of seeing him. One time, my dogs get out and somebody from Animal Control or the cops or the CIA calls me and says, "Come get your dogs."

So I get in my truck to drive one street over to pick them

up. A cop stops me. Guess what? I'm driving with a suspended license! So he writes me a ticket.

Now I'm really pissed off, and I'm trying to get my dogs in the truck, but they won't come, so I grab Ass, kinda rough.

The cop sees this and hollers, "Hey! I'll report you to the ASPCA right now and have you locked up."

At that point I'm just about to lose it. I'm about ready to cry. Soon after that day, I stopped coming out of my house.

As I moved more heavily into drugs, I shunned crowds. I'd try to get clean, sometimes, but that never lasted for long. My greatest problem was that my drug dealer lived five minutes away.

I had been doing pretty well for a couple of months, but one day he had a little party over at his house and invited me over. I used to go over there to play cards all the time, so I went over to play cards. I wish I hadn't.

A lot of people were there, and they were doing their little thing, but it wasn't affecting me. I'm playing cards, I'm not even dealing with it. They're snorting, but that didn't interest me. Once you start smoking, snorting is child's play—you don't want to waste your time with that. So I'm talking to this good-looking girl at the party and we agree to hook up back at my house.

I go home, and a few minutes later she stops by. She comes upstairs, pulls out some coke, and asks if I know how to cook it. So I cooked it up for her, and I take one little hit, just to be polite, right? That one little hit started me on a bad, bad run of who knows how long.

After that night, I started doing more shit than I had ever

done. It got to a point where I was doing it every day. My life was spiraling into a black hole. I didn't know who I was. For three or four months, I wouldn't even leave the house. All my friends were druggies. Sometimes my mother would call and I'd look at the caller ID and wouldn't even answer the phone.

PAUL DAVIS

One time he was talking about committing suicide. He knew he had a problem and didn't see a way out. He felt he had let a lot of people down.

That was the worst period I ever went through. My friends would come over and they'd find me sitting in my living room smoking crack in the middle of the afternoon, talking excitedly about some bullshit pyramid scheme. My silk curtains had been replaced with white sheets.

I was still paying my bills, but debts were piling up.

Because of my suspended license, and the fact that the cops—the same cops who used to cut me slack when I was LT—now had a hard-on for me, I was afraid to drive. I should have bought stock in McDonald's because that's about all I ate. McDonald's twice a day, every day. Double quarter-pounders. I'd sit in my room and watch the Sci-fi Channel—well, the porn channel, too—and do my drugs. I got to be skinny as hell.

One thing that didn't change was my prodigious appetite for sex. There must be Viagra in my bloodstream or something. During this period of time, I had 1-800-Call-a-Bitch on my speed dial. Within a three-month period, I spent around $70,000 on escorts. It could've been $90,000. I've always been an I-Buy-Everybody-Have-Fun-type person. It was pretty wild. When the go-go dancers are leaving their club to come to your house, you know your house is rockin'. It was like living in Grand Central Station. I'd have two girls in my room, and two more driving over. I was pulling women in through my window. I was averaging about six a day, six a night.

MARK LEPSELTER, manager

I went over to LT's house to have him sign some papers, and he comes to the door with nothing on but a towel around his waist. We're standing around, making small talk. Except for the two women on the couch, the house was empty, a mess. I ask him, "How's everything going? What have you been up to?"

And he answers me, very matter-of-factly, "Just fucking."

I had a buddy with me and LT looks at him and says, "Hey Kareem!" The guy's name is Eric, but LT doesn't care. "Hey Kareem!"

Eric answers him, "Yeah?"

"Who's the big man?"

"Uh . . ."

"Who's the big man, the big motherfucker who says he had sex with twenty thousand women and whatnot."

"Wilt Chamberlain."

"Well, you tell Wilt Chamberlain that if he takes one day off, I'm in his ass! I am in his ass!"

The sad thing was that I wasn't scared about what was happening to me. At first. But as it progressed, I started feeling doomed. You want out, but the disease won't let you out. I was also afraid of seeking help because I was so afraid of the public finding out, afraid of letting my skeletons out of the closet. And I had a graveyard full of skeletons.

I was doing more cocaine than I'd ever done before. Once you start up again, it's twice as hard to quit, and the next time it's four times as hard to quit. I felt locked in for life, to the point where I thought, "Fuck it."

KIM

He was a recluse. He even stopped playing golf. He stayed in the house all the time. I've never seen him that depressed. I've seen him play golf in the rain. It would be ten degrees and snowing outside, and he'd tell Paul Davis, "Book me a flight to where it's seventy degrees."

Paul would say, "Where?"

Lonnie would say, "I don't care. Book me a flight to where it's seventy degrees."

Paul would say, "When do you want to come back?"

Lonnie would say, "I don't know, just book me a flight to where it's seventy degrees."

Paul would book a flight, and then drive over to pick Lonnie up. And Lonnie'd go outside in his flip-flops, seven inches of snow on the ground, jump in the car, and say, "Let's roll, Paul. I have to go."

BYRON HUNT

Lawrence would be walking around the house naked, and when he got ready to go somewhere, he just put on his overcoat and a pair of flip-flops and go get in his car and take off with nothing under it. That was his driving attire, I guess.

If you weren't a dealer, an addict, or a hooker, I didn't want to know you. Addicts don't want to deal with somebody who isn't doing what they're doing. I mean, why do I want you watching me get high? It got so bad that I didn't play golf for nine months.

My friends would visit and try to help, but I didn't want to have anything to do with them.

BYRON HUNT

I'd occasionally stop by LT's Upper Saddle River home. The houses on LT's street were just immaculate. You wouldn't know anything was going on in his house until you stepped inside. I couldn't believe what I saw. First off, there was a naked girl sitting downstairs. When I went upstairs, I found LT in the bedroom having a senseless argument with another girl. I'd be sitting there having a cold beer just talking shop. The skin flicks are going . . . but it's a minor distraction. It's just part of the whole scenery.

The place was a mess. Lawrence was never a good housekeeper, so naturally, when he lived by himself, it had

gotten worse. I remember the dogs hadn't been let out. There was crap all over the place. The thing I remember most of all is the burns from when he smoked cocaine; he was putting it in a cigarette, so naturally, there were a lot of cigarette burns. The bed, the carpet, all over the place.

And all I remember was thinking, "He's gotta be getting close to a breaking point." He was hanging with people you'd avoid on Forty-second Street, you know what I'm saying? I just knew at some point he was gonna wake up and say, "You know what? This is ridiculous. I can't be doing this."

BOBBY CUPO

If you walked into his house, it was a crack house. I'd been told horror stories by a Giant fan known as Pizza Man, who would deliver steaks to Lawrence. The Pizza Man says to me, "I could not wait to get out of the house." He said there were drug addicts laying in the corner curled up in a ball.

Yes, the rugs were burned, but he also had a hole knocked into one of the walls so he could crawl into the bedrooms. I don't know why it was there.

Rock bottom was coming, coming as fast and as hard as I used to turn the corner, looking to nail a quarterback.

CHAPTER THIRTEEN

Nineteen ninety-eight was what you might call a banner year, especially if that banner was made in hell. I was arrested three times: once for failing to pay child support and twice on drug-related charges. In October, I checked into a rehab center after being arrested for trying to buy crack from an undercover officer in St. Pete, Florida. In December, I surrendered to Teaneck, New Jersey, police to face charges of possession of narcotics and paraphernalia. I also filed for bankruptcy to keep creditors from taking my house in Upper Saddle River.

St. Petersburg. Once again, it was setup. Just like the one in Myrtle Beach. I'm not saying I was a virgin, but it was still a setup.

I was down in St. Petersburg, playing in a golf tournament. The local cops had caught some guy who had sold crack to a friend of mine, and this guy—big surprise—thought he could get off if he handed me to the cops. Sound familiar?

It was a bullshit setup—an elaborate, messy bit of entrapment, my lawyer says—but I was busted. My friend and I rented a car and went looking for an area where her ex-husband lived, but we couldn't find the address. I asked this dude walking his dog and he's like, "I can't tell you, but I'll show you." Okay, fine, we're driving and my friend asked the dogwalker if he knows where to get some coke. The guy said he does. I never asked this guy, 'cause I don't know the sonuvabitch.

A couple hours later, I was back at the hotel and there's a phone call. It's the dogwalker. "I got some shit here," he said, "some fifty-dollar pieces they're selling for twenty. Aren't you gonna take these off my hands?" I told him, "Nah, man, I'm cool, I don't want anything." So we hung up.

Then he called back again twice, being real persistent, and I told him that I'd pick him up at the place we met. But I didn't go anywhere. I was very uncomfortable at this point and I didn't want anything to do with this guy. But, sure enough, he calls again, asking where I was, and I told him there were too many cops and I had to just leave. So, get this, he said he'll come to my place. I told him, "No, forget it. I don't like the situation, man. I don't want to deal with it." It was now about ten P.M. and I'd had enough. I took the phone off the hook. Then, at about two in the morning, there's a knock at my door. I look outside the window and I see this girl standing there. Pretty decent–looking girl. And I'm damn naked. I look around the corner and there's the dogwalker. "Oh, open the door, motherfucker, open the door," he said.

I opened the door. "It's two o'clock in the morning, what

the hell you doing here?" I said. They come into the room and I'm looking at this girl, thinking, "Damn, maybe my boy brought me some pussy." I'd put on a towel by now, and my lady friend is wide awake and we're sitting on the bed. He said, "Man, I want you to look at this shit." I told him, "Man, look, I'm tired. I gotta get up early."

They tried to sell me some shit and I kept telling them to come back tomorrow. I figured I'd be flying out tomorrow, they'd show up, I wouldn't be there, and it'd be over. Then the girl said, "I can't come back because I have to work." She turned to the dogwalker and said, "You told me I'm gonna get me some money, you know we ain't got no gas, and the kids need milk." She looked at me again. "You telling me you can't give me something for gas or anything? I drove all the way over here."

Well, I had nothing but hundreds in my pants. So my friend gave me a fifty. I gave it to the girl, and the guy said, "Let him check out some of the big ones, give him the big one." She shows me this rock, I put it in my hand and she said, "You keep that for this."

"All right, whatever. Cool." Then the door crashes open and the cops come running in and they got me for purchasing fifty dollars' worth of crack.

I sat in the back of the police car, humiliated, handcuffs behind my back. The ride to Pinellas County Jail took half an hour, but it seemed to last all night. Once again, they were nice to me at the jail, asked for autographs and stuff like that. They even put me in a cell by myself, and really took care of me. I had to find a lawyer, then arrange for bail. I was over at

the bail bondsman's office all day, fightin' off the press and everything. Then I had to bail my lady friend out. It wasn't until the next afternoon, after I'd posted a $15,500 bond, that we were able to leave. Then I went to see a lawyer and he said, "That's entrapment."

I still could not believe they arrested me. I didn't say anything in the transcripts—yes, the punk-ass was wired—that would incriminate me. Still, I pleaded no contest because they promised me that I'd just get probation.

This time I didn't get to fly back to Newark on a private jet. This time I flew commercial. Seemed like everybody on the plane knew who I was. Just some more good ol' fucking humiliation.

HARRY CARSON

George Martin and I knew everybody was gonna dwell on the whole drug-bust thing. We were trying to meet with him to get him involved in some positive things. We wanted to meet him face-to-face to sit down with him to talk about what we wanted to do. We were concerned about his reputation.

The meeting never happened.

Once I got home, there was more bad news. In September of '98, cops had found crack cocaine and narcotics paraphernalia in a room that was rented in my name at a Marriott in Teaneck, New Jersey. I wasn't in the room. How can they arrest me for drug paraphernalia if they can't even place me in that room? They did anyway.

They charged me with it, though not on the day they found the stuff in that room, not the next day, not even the next week. They charged me a month later, which is bullshit. They didn't charge me until after I got busted in Florida. At that point, it was a free-for-all, I guess, and everybody was trying to get on the bandwagon. I guess the New Jersey cops were pissed off that only Florida cops were getting to arrest LT.

I didn't even show up for the trial. I think they charged me with a misdemeanor. I wasn't living full-time in Jersey anymore, so I didn't give a shit what they did. I paid the $1,100 fine because the appeal would have cost me $5,000. I wasn't going to sit there in court and put on no show for them.

One more kick in the ass in '98: The cops came to my home at two A.M. and arrested me on a deadbeat-dad raid. I was hauled to jail for failing to pay child support on time. That was the biggest sham, because I was only a month behind, but they sent eleven cops to my house in the middle of the night.

I had to try to sleep on a hard bed in the jail cell until nine o'clock, till the magistrate came in. I just had to pay $400 and I was free to go. My wife hadn't filed any charges against me. She had no problem with me. A week later, the cop who arrested me got arrested for being $11,000 in arrears.

I had come back home from Florida after my arrest in St. Petersburg on a Monday. I had a meeting with the feds on Tuesday. They were going to put me in protective custody

because they didn't want me getting in any more trouble and mess up their case—they were counting on me to be a witness against my former partner in LT's, Al Porro. Porro would eventually be convicted of embezzlement, money laundering, bank fraud, and tax evasion. They didn't put me in jail, but they did tell me I had to check into Honesty House by seven o'clock that night. And stay there.

I thought I was going to be in there for two weeks, which I didn't think was a bad deal. I met with Bill and Charlie as soon as I got to Honesty House. Right off the bat, Charlie and I were cussin' each other out. I told him, "This is bullshit. I shouldn't be in here."

MARK LEPSELTER

I'd just gotten the script for Oliver Stone's movie *Any Given Sunday*, and they had a role for LT. So I sent him the script and he freaked because he was worried he'd lose the role while in rehab. But they were nice enough to give him a couple days' exception so he could do a screen test.

I moped around for the first two or three days. Finally, Charlie called me into his office and said, "Are you ready to start getting something done? 'Cause whenever you're ready, that's when we're going to start the time." This was my moment of truth. "You're not here for two weeks," Charlie told me. "You're here for thirty days." And that thirty days didn't start until I started really working the program.

I was so pissed off I didn't do anything for another two

days. I'd been there for almost a week, and my time hadn't even started yet. After wasting a couple of more days feeling sorry for myself, I finally got off my ass and started getting with the program. I went to the in-house meetings, and the breakfasts. Charlie got me a roommate—first time I've ever had one. He said I could choose who I wanted, but I was going to get a roommate, either way. The honeymoon was over for me—I had to start following rules like everybody else. I couldn't skip meetings like I used to. I had to go to the outside meetings. I did homework. I filled out a report after each lesson. I even started talking in the group sessions.

I was a little depressed, though. I remember sitting on the steps outside Honesty House talking quietly to Lauren Schoonover, who worked there with her dad. I was telling her about my ex, how I now realized that it was me who had destroyed that relationship. I told Lauren sadly, "All she ever wanted was for me to be a husband."

After I'd been in Honesty House for thirty days, I packed my shit. I was ready to go home, but Charlie came in and told me, "You can't leave for another thirty days." He said it was the feds' call.

I had a choice: I could be mad at Charlie (and the feds), or I could get something out of the program while I was there. I decided to get something out of it.

Bob tells people that the breakthrough came for me after he showed one of my game tapes to the whole group. I don't remember much about it, but Bob swears I had been bragging that I kicked ass even when I was doing coke. What I saw on that game film humbled me. I told him, "I never realized it was that bad." It looked like I was running underwater.

When I stood in front of a group and said, "My name is Lawrence, and I'm an addict," I believed it this time. I had never believed it before. I'm a recovering addict, and I'll be an addict till the day I die. And it doesn't embarrass me.

Now, I didn't mind telling my story. I used to hate listening to people's stories, because it almost always became a lying contest: "Oh, you think *you* were bad, I used to do such and such . . ." People want to make their story *sooooo* entertaining. But I began to see why you have to tell your story.

Fighting the Enemy is just like every other big challenge in your life. You need a plan. You don't go into a football game without having a game plan and knowing who you're playing. You don't go into a battle without knowing something about who you're fighting. But so many people get into drugs not knowing what they're messing with. What you have to do to get sober.

And that's what I tried to relay by telling my story: You think you're bad? I've done *bam-bam-bam* . . . But I could never get clean. What I was trying to illustrate to my fellow addicts was that you may not get it the first time, you may not get it the second time, you may not get it the third time. Sooner or later, though, if you stick with it, you're going to get it. You have to be patient. Anybody who tries to get sober is thinking: "How the fuck am I going to be sober for the rest of my life? That's a *long* time." But I don't think that way. No. I think, "I just have to stay sober till tomorrow."

I had been there for two months now. I became the senior member of the house! It gave me a sense of responsibility. We always had newcomers coming in, and I had to show 'em the ropes. It got to the point where I could teach the lessons, run the meetings.

If nobody else wanted to start the meetings, I had no problem doing it. The counselors would give all of us little jobs. You have to sweep the dining room, you have to set the tables or mop the floors, or clean the chalkboard, or you'd have to make the coffee. The first two times there, I didn't do none of that shit. This time, I was just like any other member of the house. I liked cooking the best. I made pork chops and mashed potatoes. The program was facing budgetary cutbacks, so I bought the food I cooked for everybody with my own money. The people in that house became my family, and the staff treated me with a lot of dignity. The staff let me out for golf on a Saturday, if it was a slow day. I donated a StairMaster and weights. We had volleyball games, we had a Ping-Pong championship, we had a little band. I even learned to play a little piano. When someone's in detox, it's important to get their blood sugar up, so I'd go out and buy candy. I'd walk around Honesty House carrying a Snickers or a Butterfingers, and pass it out to whoever needed one. Once again, I was the Candy Man. Strictly a nonprofit thing this time.

I wasn't your ordinary run-of-the-mill addict. I signed plenty of autographs in there. When the families came, I had to meet mothers and fathers and sisters, girlfriends. It didn't bother me. Hey, the whole world knew I was there. I even let a couple of young girls put makeup on me one night—red lipstick, blue eye shadow, mascara. "I'll let you do it," I told them, "but don't tell anybody." It wasn't easy getting that shit off, believe me.

That group became really close—we still call each other to this day. "How is Wes doing? How is Cathy doing?" A lot of them have been back to Honesty House. One guy has been there five or six times; he's doing great now.

You see everything at a place like Honesty House. You see people go into seizures. You see thieves. There are no fences around Honesty House. If you don't want to be there, you just open the door and walk out. I've seen people jump ship. One guy who had been there a couple of times had a fuss with his girlfriend, so he mixed a half a gallon of vodka and antifreeze. He was back in Honesty House two days after he got out of the hospital. It's like a little Peyton Place.

I used to go to a police officers' AA meeting on Thursday nights. All of the cops were either alcoholics or addicts, and man, some of their stories made me look like a church mouse.

Why did it work this time? Because it wasn't a question of me just being there. It wasn't, "Okay, LT, you have to be in this place for twenty-eight days," or "LT, you have to be there for ten days." No. I was going to be there until I started working the program.

What I finally got from Charlie's lectures was that you had to do things for yourself, give yourself small moments of joy. He used to have fresh-cut flowers on his desk, and treat himself to Chinese food on Thursday nights. I play golf.

Charlie also taught us that everyone has the same five needs. The first one is to love and be loved. The second human need is to achieve. The third is for freedom. (Charlie says that the power people have to hurt you is the power that you have given them.) The fourth human need is to take care of your own body—proper nutrition, proper frame of mind. For example, anger can ruin your immune system, and resentment is a luxury that people in recovery can't afford to have. The fifth human need is spirituality, a belief in something higher than yourself.

What was the difference between me sitting in Honesty House two years earlier saying, "Damn, I don't want to do this shit no more" and then going back and getting high the very next day, and being sober now? I think the answer is that you won't get better until you are sick and tired of being sick and tired. Then you have to put some time between you and whatever you're doing, whether you're drinking or getting high. I remember telling Charlie, "I just want to be able to put myself in a position to make a choice again." When I was smoking crack, I had no choice. The drug made my choices for me. Charlie, the program, and the camaraderie of my group gave me a chance to make a choice.

I had just come off a period of time where my confidence was shot. I didn't know who I was. And I was doing some things I'd never thought I'd do. And it's not what you think.

RUSS FABER, sports agent

I set LT up with hotel arrangements and Disney attraction tickets, and now he had to ride in the parade. He thought he was gonna sit in the car and wave. Disney came out with an Aladdin costume with pointed shoes. They gave it to me and expected me to give it to him: "Oh, by the way, they want you to wear this little thing."

He looked at me and said, "What the fuck is this?" He thought I was joking with him. "They'd like you to walk along the route," I told him. In an Aladdin genie outfit with all these little gadgets hanging from him. After I got him in the suit, they gave me a hat to put on him. Like a wizard hat. So now, I got him dressed head to toe looking like a genie. His family was in the VIP seating watching the parade, so he can't back out now. They're expecting him in the car.

As the parade was starting to roll out, the Disney people come up to me 'cause they see him chewing Skoal. He can't spit on Main Street, it's not good for the Disney image. I said to Lawrence, "I owe you big for this: Do you mind not dipping?" He kinda said, "Screw that, I'll just swallow it." He kept dipping, and instead of spitting, he just swallowed.

Nobody tells him what to do. It was like he was in a game. He was like Showtime. You would never know he was embarrassed or shy or pissed. He walked into the crowd, taking pictures as he was walking. His family thought it was the greatest thing.

But, over time, I began getting my confidence back and *boom! boom!* I had things rolling over here, rolling over there. Oliver Stone called me, and said, "If you get clean, brother, I'd like to have you in my movie." That's how I got my role in *Any Given Sunday*. Things started to happen for me again.

Filming is tedious work. I'd keep doing a scene over and over and over again. They wanted to show the hits from different angles. They wanted to see dramatic hits. It's gotta be head-to-head, helmet-to-helmet. I wanted to do the hits myself, and even though I don't do a lot of helmet-to-helmet, especially at my age now, I did it for the movie. I remember catching him—Ricky's coming over the top, I'm coming over the top. I used to get burners all the time when I was in the NFL, and boy, I caught one of those shots, I thought I was gonna have to be carried off the field. Very very painful. I let the double do the work from that point on. If they didn't have to see the face, I wasn't gonna do the hitting.

RICKY WATTERS, running back, actor

I didn't understand how movies go. I was out there running fast, I'm running people over, and everybody's like, "Hold on here. You need to calm down because we're gonna make you look fast. You don't have to run so fast, you know?" LT had to do more than me. He had to jam a guy, he had to spin off and then make a play on me here. I'm coming already full speed, and I just think we hit too hard. It was a play he's supposed to stay down. So we were like,

"Wow, he's acting so great, he's still down!" All of a sudden we're like, "He's not getting up," and he wasn't about to get up. And so everybody was realizing what had happened. I guess he had a pinched nerve or something. Of course everybody was blowing it out of proportion and making it this big thing and I'm like, "C'mon, man, don't get me on LT's bad side."

One of the biggest things about to happen for me was being inducted into the Pro Football Hall of Fame. Everybody agreed that I was a lock to be voted in the second I became eligible. Well, almost everybody. Some know-nothings in the press and on the radio said I shouldn't be in the Hall of Fame because of my drug problems. I thought that was stupid. Hell, I wasn't trying to get into the AA Hall of Fame.

Even the cops were treating me better now. I was driving on the Garden State heading to Atlantic City for an alcoholism conference when I got pulled over for, what else, speeding. The cop recognizes me and says, "Oh, sorry to inconvenience you," and lets me go. So I turn on my music and I'm back on the road, doing 85 mph.

After about two minutes, I see lights flashing in my rearview mirror. I pull over. It's the same cop, so I figure I'm screwed. He walks up to my window and says, "Can I get your autograph?" I didn't know whether to laugh or cry.

When I walked out of Honesty House that last time, I had to go to the federal courthouse to deal with my IRS problems. And as soon as I got out of federal court, the feds slapped a monitor on my leg and I was under house arrest for another twenty days. I had to be back in the house by eight o'clock every day.

IRIS

When I went up and saw my son under house arrest, it tore me apart. I knew even with that, God was going to bring him out. I do believe God has angels.

I should have been depressed, but I felt different this time. I was doing the movie *Any Given Sunday* (started filming January '99), and I'd signed to host FX's *Toughman* show for 2000, 2001, and 2002, so I told myself, "You got another chance here, homeboy. Make sure you don't fuck it up."

MATT VASGERSIAN, *Toughman* announcer

One of the first fights we were doing, one of the guys that was fighting I believe was 515 pounds. His nickname was Highlander; he wore a kilt. It was early in the show and LT was kinda tentative when to come in. I looked at LT and said, "Look at this guy. He's five hundred and something pounds, he's huge, he can't move at all. You'd think maybe he'd want to go on the Atkins diet." And LT says, "I went on one of those high-protein, low-carb diets. You don't eat no bread. You eat twelve whole motherfucking chickens. You ain't gonna lose no weight." The next thing I hear in my ear is the control room laughing their ass off. The next voice was the producer: "LT, what part of twelve

whole motherfucking chickens do you think we'll be able to use for the show?" He's one of the funniest guys I've ever been around.

He had three or four canned responses to what would happen. One was, "Here, take that witcha!" Another was, "Somebody call the cops, there's gonna be a murder!" A third one was, "That's what I'm talkin' about!" And "Looky here, looky here." And then he wouldn't follow it up with anything.

One time Rickey Jackson started throwing up and they needed a replacement, so I climbed into the ring to fight Ickey Woods, who at 275 outweighed me by 25 pounds. The pressure was on. I mean, if I lost, how was I gonna look being the announcer and all? I went in there (Rickey loaned me his shorts and Gary Reasons his size 13 shoes), and I'm looking for that hi sign that says, "Hey, we're just gonna brother-in-law this shit." I can't get no sign. Ickey was just looking at me dead straight in the eye. I'm like, "Oh shit."

So we get in the ring and we're just bouncing around, bouncing around, bouncing around; that sonuvabitch hit me square in the face. I didn't even see the "Toughman" written on the glove. Hell, I didn't even see the glove. I saw the *O* and the *U* and the *G* when it got right in front of my nose. That sonuvabitch knocked me through the ropes and then he started to whale on me. My legs just went completely like rubber. And I'm saying to myself—this is where I guess all my football training came in—"LT, whatever you do, you can't hit this floor." So I got enough energy to fight him off me, and we just danced the rest of that round. But he really hurt me pretty good. Then I won the second round and the third round, we were just playing around, and I thought, "I'm just gonna wait till the last ten seconds and then *bam, bam, bam!*" I can go for ten seconds. So at the end of the round, I tore his ass off. I watched a lot of Ali's fights, and if it's close, if you come out strong the last ten seconds, then usually you're gonna win the fight.

ICKEY WOODS

I think I took him by surprise in the first round 'cause I jumped on him real fast. I had him dazed there a little bit. My adrenaline was really going and I pushed him into the ropes and he went halfway through. So the ref backed me off him and I think that gave him time to recoup. Probably with about eight seconds left in the third round, he caught me with a little shot that stumbled me back a little bit. By the time I recovered, the bell rang. Going into the fight, I knew if I didn't knock him out, I wasn't gonna get the decision. Why? Because it was his show!

A year later I fought Hugh Green and knocked him out in the second round. But sorry, baby, don't expect any more *Toughman* fights from me. I'm getting too old for that kinda shit.

One of the best things I did was to move to Florida. I got away from all the bad shit in my bad life. A fresh start. Of

course I have regrets. I lost a lot of years there where I didn't get to watch my children grow. I can never get those years back, but one of the things I'm proudest of is that my kids have hung in there with me.

I've given millions away, millions. I'm the type of person, if I got five dollars and you ask me for six, I'll find a way to get the other dollar. It's like, "Can I borrow fifty thousand dollars?" And I'll say, "I tell you what: I'll give you twenty-five thousand dollars." I feel this way—if they don't pay you back, they never can ask you again.

I never made a big deal about all the charity stuff I did when I was playing, going to hospitals and burn centers and stuff like that. When I'm in Miami, I like to hang out with homeless people. I take 'em food, take 'em clothes, sit there and bullshit with 'em. I'm no different than them. I have problems just like they do. And they aren't quick to judge a person for things he's done wrong.

I like to give things to people in need. My assistant Vicki was driving me to an autograph signing once and we were late, but I told her to pull over. I went into an army-navy store and came out with a big cardboard box and jammed it in the back of the Land Rover. She drove me to a schoolyard where I had seen these kids with ragged clothes playing basketball. I got out and threw the box onto that court. "Drive away," I told her.

As we pulled off, I could see those kids pulling coats out of the box.

MEL JONES

Lawrence has never forgotten his high school. He has probably given us, over the years, $100,000 toward scholarships to help the kids at Lafayette. He has sent me money for uniforms. He's a giver.

I'm Lawrence Taylor now, but LT still surfaces from time to time. Sometimes within the same damn minute. As one of my friends put it: "I love to see LT coming, and I love to see him leave!"

CHAPTER FOURTEEN

I n 1999, six years after I had retired from the Giants, I experienced my best moment as a football player. I was inducted into the Hall of Fame.

I thought the debate over whether or not I should be in the Hall of Fame was idiotic. If I didn't belong in the Hall of Fame, then who did? The Hall of Fame isn't about what you do off the field, it's what you do on the field. Where does it say in the bylaws that you can't have any problems in your life? Hell, half of the sportswriters who vote for the Hall of Fame are drunks.

Getting in made me think about how lucky I had been in my career. Not that I didn't have a lot of talent, and bust my ass on the field, but I knew I'd been lucky to have been drafted by a team with great leaders like Harry Carson and George Martin. They were the guys Bill would turn to—if there was a problem, he would tell Harry and George to fix it.

Harry and I had a couple of problems, basically because I think he was jealous of my success. Before I came to New

York, Harry was The Man, he was Mr. Defense for the Giants, and all of a sudden I became Mr. Defense. That was a source of tension that built up over the years, but when I first got there, I was a toddler, just following behind Dad, and that was Harry Carson. He showed me the ropes. We'd have our own little parties and just sit back and talk. When you sit down and talk to Harry, you're in for a treat, because he's very knowledgeable.

I learned to trust Harry on the football field. Our more serious problems started after he retired. A lot of players think that when they do commentary on television or radio, the best way to make your name is to be negative. I think that's what Harry did. Every time the media wanted something negative about the Giants, they'd call Harry. It bothered me because he fought in the trenches with us for a lot of years, and all of a sudden he was selling us down the river. I couldn't understand it. After one of my drug episodes, Harry had more negative things to say, and Harry and I finally had it out, face-to-face. It wasn't pretty, that's all I'll say about it. I didn't talk to Harry for quite a while after that.

HARRY CARSON

LT was doing a TV interview following his retirement, and when they asked him about his finances, he lashed into me for whatever reason. He started talking about me and how I was jealous of him. I really didn't know where that came from. I could see by looking at his face that he was in the midst of a furious drug battle, and felt for him. I held

fire. He's my brother. Even though I might be angry with my brother about something, I'm not going to discard my brother. We went through a lot together. You don't just callously throw a relationship away. It would have taken much more than that to sever our relationship, although it was strained. I would never have allowed it to sever.

It takes a big man to rise above petty shit like that, and Harry Carson is a big man. I was thrilled when he showed up to share my day at the Hall of Fame induction ceremony in Canton, Ohio. When Chris Berman, who was the master of ceremonies that day, introduced him to the crowd, I stood up so that I could see him.

HARRY CARSON

I stood up and made a gesture toward Lawrence. I pointed to my heart and then I pointed to him just to say, "I love you."

After the ceremony, we got together in the reception area. We didn't really say anything, we just embraced. Lawrence and I stood there—it had to be like three or four minutes—and he started crying. We were just standing there in the middle of the floor, and nobody said a word. It was as if we were just there, the two of us, in our own little world. When we unlocked, I could see Lawrence had tears in his eyes. Then T.J. came over, and the three of us stood there, and then we hugged some more. Afterward, Lawrence's ex-wife, Linda, came over to me and she said, "Thanks for coming, he really needed this."

I was embarrassed that I had let some bullshit come between our friendship. I felt like a fool for having ever doubted Harry Carson's friendship.

That was a very emotional day for me, for many reasons. In the weeks prior to the ceremony, I had to pick someone to present me at the Hall of Fame induction, and I had been having a hard time choosing between Bill Parcells and Wellington Mara. Mr. Mara, remember—and Bill and George Young—did a lot behind the scenes to help me. Mr. Mara thought I was the Ultimate Giant; I call him the Ultimate Owner. My son T.J. solved the dilemma when he asked me if he could do it.

The crowd floored me that day in Canton. There were so many LT fans wearing my jersey, chanting "LT! LT! LT!" And then T.J. walked up to the podium, and he spoke very well.

I remember telling Bill beforehand, "One thing I ain't going to do, I ain't going to cry." But as soon as T.J. finished, I stood up to hug him and I almost lost it. I was very, very proud. There are so many sons who don't give a shit about their dad. Running through my mind while I was listening to him was all the grief I'd put my family through. But T.J. still respects me, still loves me, and he's willing to tell the whole world how he feels about his dad. It's my book, and I want to print his speech, so here it is:

I would like to begin by saying today is a wonderful day. Today is the day we put my father, who I think is the greatest linebacker of all time, to the place where he belongs, the Pro Football Hall of Fame. A man who was such a domi-

nant force he changed the way the game was played. Today is the day we put my father into the place where legends live, the Pro Football Hall of Fame. It's with great pride and pleasure that I'm able to stand before you today to present such a great person, friend, and father. When I was young growing up in New Jersey, I knew my dad was special, but not only to me, but to other people . . . When I reached my teens and I read about all his accomplishments on the field, and his mishaps off the field, it helped me know, love, and respect my father even more. Those stories made me understand why people admire him so much. Sure I admired him, too—not because of LT the football player, 'cause of Lawrence Taylor, my father.

I love my father. I would do anything for him just as well as he would do anything for me, or my sisters, Whitney, Tanisha, and Paula. If I pick anybody to be my father, I'd pick Lawrence Taylor every time. Me and my father have a good relationship, we talk all the time one-on-one. We go to the movies, go bowling. Just spending time together with him is very special to me, and very special to him, too. He's not only a friend to me, he's a friend to my friends as well, because he knows how special friends are . . . My father wants the best for me just as well as his parents wanted the best for him growing up in Williamsburg, Virginia.

Most of all, I would like to just say thank you to my father for being there for me and never letting me settle for less. And even though he might not admit it, I thank Ron Jaworski for making my father what he is, 'cause without him, he probably woulda never broken that sack record!

And on behalf of my father, I will thank you, the fans in New York, the fans here in Cleveland, for lighting a fire that was in my father when he played. And like he says, without you, there would have been a Lawrence Taylor, but there would not have been an LT, and I thank you for that. So before I bring my father up here, can I hear the LT chant?

The crowd erupted: "LT! LT! LT! LT!"

IRIS

It just brought tears to my eyes. Lonnie's just a different type of dad, that's all. He wasn't one of those nine-to-five, stay-at-home dads. But he always wanted the best for his children.

It would have been impossible for me to top my son, but I had to step up to that podium and say something. Here's what I said:

I had a bet with Bill Parcells that I wouldn't cry, but he almost won the bet just now because I almost lost it.

When I first came out here today, the program was about to begin and I was a little bit nervous. The excitement was running through my head, and I was a little nervous. Then I saw all those Giants uniforms in the crowd, all the Giants stuff, and I knew that I was in LT territory and I loved it. Thank you.

It's a pleasure and an honor and I do understand what it

means to be in the Football Hall of Fame. I'm going in with a lot of great guys, and there are a lot of guys who have gone before me.

I sit back and I try to think of how I got here—it was not just through my play, because that's God-given talent, that's working with a lot of great teammates, great individuals. When I look around I see that I have to thank so many people.

First of all I want to thank the Giant fans: everybody in the NFL has great ability, we all can run, tackle, hit. But if we have no one to cheer for us, it's not worth a thing.

I have a lot of friends here today: Giants friends, personal friends. I have D'Fellas from Williamsburg, Virginia, where I grew up, and I have friends from New Jersey: Gary Gaglioti, Dino, Eric, Vicki. She is the most important thing right now to me simply because she gets everything done for me. My life is very chaotic, as you can tell, and without her working every day, I couldn't do it. Thank you, thank you very much. I have cousins . . . cousins and cousins and cousins and cousins and cousins.

I'd also like to thank my teammates, some of whom are here today. O. J. Anderson, Gary Jeter, George Martin . . . And let me tell you about one other teammate here today. This guy and I had some words a while back, we kinda parted ways, and we didn't talk. But I'll tell ya, Harry Carson came out for me today, and that's the classiest thing I've ever seen in my life, Harry. Thank you, thank you. I love you, man. I love you.

I want to thank Lauren and her dad, his wife, and my best friend in the whole world, Paul Davis, and his wife; he's been with me for a lot of years. I'd like to thank my family for being here with me. My mom and my dad; my two brothers, Clarence and Kim, and his [Kim's] wife and kids. My loving ex-wife—seriously—Linda Taylor. Stand up, girl. There are my in-laws. My ex–in-laws . . . Even though they're my exes, I still love 'em. I love 'em all.

I'd like to thank my kids for understanding that people make mistakes in life. And somehow they have the ability to forgive me and love me anyway, and I thank them for that.

Three people in my football career have been really instrumental. One of those men is George Young. When he drafted me, a lot of people asked him why—until they saw the tapes. George has always been in my corner, he's always helped me push to do better . . . to stay out of trouble . . . to do the right thing. George has always been there for me, and I'd like to thank him.

There's another man who was very important. You talk about the George Halases, you talk about the Paul Browns, you talk about all the great owners in the league . . . Let me tell you something, you're committing an injustice if you don't talk about Wellington Mara. All you Giant fans know that Wellington Mara really loves his football team. He stood behind me for a lot of years on the field and off the field. Without him, I probably would not be here today. So I want to thank Wellington Mara for his kindness and generosity. Thank you, Wellington.

And I'd like to thank a coach, Bill Parcells. He's the coach of coaches, in my opinion. I have never had a coach who knew football as well, who knew me as well, and was able to *put the two together and make a great combination. I was asked about Bill, do we talk anymore? Well, it's like a marriage that's lasted thirty years—you don't talk as much as you used to, but you know you love each other anyway. Without Bill Parcells, I would not have been able to do the things I was able to do.*

And lastly, people ask me all the time, what kind of legacy do you want to leave behind? And I thought about that, and it's indeed a great honor to be here, but I think I want to leave all the people this: Life, like anything else, can knock you down, it can turn you out . . . you have problems every day in your life. But sometimes, as Ozzie Newsome said earlier, some days, you just have to go play. You just have to go play.

And no matter how many times it knocks you down, no matter how many times you think you can't go forward, no matter how many times things just don't go right . . . Anybody can quit. Anybody can do that.

A Hall of Famer never quits.

A Hall of Famer realizes that the crime is not being knocked down, the crime is not getting up again.

And I want to thank you for allowing me to be here. Thank you very much.

Beasley didn't write that one. That bad boy was all mine.

IRIS

I had flashbacks of him and his brothers playing with the dog. That dog thought he was one of the kids, so they taught him how to play football. And they would put shots and a T-shirt on him.

LINDA

I earned that Hall of Fame just like he did. I wasn't on the field, but I fought all the battles he fought. Right now, he's in such a better place, the best Lawrence has been. This is the Lawrence I fell in love with.

WHITNEY TAYLOR DAVIS

It's been a long journey with my father, and it's not over yet. He's been through a lot of things, from being famous to being into drugs, that took a toll on a lot of people's relationships with him. A lot of times I'm not sure if my father feels maybe guilty for not being there as much as he should. A lot of times I wanted to be with my father to have just regular father-daughter conversations. But I was so proud of him that day at the Hall of Fame.

T.J.

I couldn't be happier. Dad just has a new focus on what he wants to do. He's changed his life totally around. He

seems a lot happier, he looks better, and when we're around each other he has a lot more energy. He has somebody in his life now that makes him happy. As long as he's happy, I'm happy.

Maybe the best thing that happened to me was I may have finally found the right girl. I met Maritza on the set of *Any Given Sunday,* during my first nonfootball scene. She was one of the extras. When I shook her hand, I slipped her a piece of paper with my phone number. I asked her to call me in the morning. She waited a day before she called. When she did finally call, we made a date to have dinner together.

We went to a Vietnamese restaurant. I didn't recognize anything on the menu, so I tried to cover by saying, "You order whatever you're going to have, I'll just watch you eat."

Maritza's not a football fan, so she couldn't understand why people were coming over for my autograph. I told her that I used to play for the New York Giants and left it at that. She had plans later that night and asked me to join her and her friends. I told her, "No, I don't go out to clubs." But of course I changed my mind. We hung out till 2:30.

We hit it off, and after about four months I asked her to come with me to Williamsburg to visit my father. While we were there, we took a walk through my old town and then sat on a bench, where I started telling her about my life. I told her I had broken up with my fiancée and had just gotten out of rehab. I told her, "I want to change my life. I want to try to be the best I can. I know I've messed up in my life. I'd rather tell you than have you hear it from somebody else." Unbeknownst to me, she had already heard it from somebody else. I told her I was serious about her. She says that was the night she fell in love with me.

Maritza stood on the sidelines with me during the NFC championship game in December 2000—Giants 41, Vikings 0. When she started shivering, I grabbed one of the players' warm-up jackets and draped it over her. The crowd went "Awwwwwww." You can bet no one inside Giants Stadium had ever seen *that* side of LT.

After about three months, we became engaged. In June of 2001, I came back to Miami after a business trip and told Maritza, "I brought something for you." I handed her a jewelry box. She thought I'd bought her some earrings.

Maritza started hyperventilating. She said, "Is this a joke?"

I put the ring on her finger. "Now," I said, "you're officially off the market."

Okay, so I'm not *always* bad with rings. We got married in South Beach on November 28, 2001. She's Puerto Rican, and hotheaded. I spend a lot of my time now dodging bullets. I think she is one of the best things to happen to me, and probably one of the worst. Every day is a little bit of drama, but I do love her and she loves me.

MARITZA TAYLOR

The past four years, I can't begin to tell you how much gray I've got in my hair! Living with Taylor, it just makes you turn gray instantaneously. We can't live without each other, and

we can't live with each other. It's both at the same time.
Life with Lawrence Taylor is a roller-coaster ride.

She's never seen me play. I like that. She has never read my press clippings. All she knows is who I am now. I have a clean slate with her. I never want her to see that ugly side of me. She's never seen me out on the streets. And I'm not going to let her see me like that.

IRIS

If there is such a thing as hell, Lonnie's been through it. He achieved what he wanted as far as playing ball, but with all of that, the way he was when I saw him last year at his daughter's graduation is most important. He looked happy. He could have been faking it—he's good at it—but he was calm and he was enjoying the children. It's time that some good things happen for him.

A long time ago, Ivery told me, "It's not important who you love; what's important is who loves you." I didn't understand what that was all about back then. I understand it now. The people I deal with now don't know the ugly part of my life. All they know is who I am now.

Who am I? I've been to hell and back. Who am I now? I'm not an angry person anymore. I like the lifestyle I have now. I don't need pats on the back, but it always surprises me how many people still show me respect. It always amazes me that after all I've been through—and all I've put people through—people still hold me in high regard. It's a good feeling.

I've been lucky enough to get my foot in a lot of doors. I do have the acting bug. I've played a transvestite, Fighting Iris, in the Showtime *Going to California* series. When my agent, Mark Lepselter, told me about the part, I said, "No, no, no! I got a cousin who's half a fag, but ol' LT ain't gonna play no fag." I called Vicki and she said, "You've done everything else, why not a woman?" So I called Mark back and accepted the role. Hey—it shows my range, right?

This may sound conceited, but I'm impressed with myself. Four years ago, I would have said I was in too deep. I saw no way out. The people at Honesty House helped me see that there was a light at the end of the tunnel. At first, it wasn't a big light—I could barely see it. Now it's my sunshine.

Who knows what would have happened to me if I hadn't pulled out of it? The Enemy was telling me where to go, when to sleep, when to eat . . . everything. I'd probably be dead.

I'm certain that my football background helped save me. You have to have a game plan. When I started putting my problem into football terms—offense, defense, game plan, having a strong head coach, which was Charlie—then I had a chance. I still do that to this day. You have to have a game plan for everything.

Golf will always be a big part of my game plan. A friend built a three-hole golf course on his ten-acre farm in Wachung, New Jersey. Real ritzy neighborhood. One day I stopped by. It was a hot summer day, and I showed up wearing this eggplant-colored suit. Their tractor was sitting in the parking lot. "Do you mind if I take it for a spin?" I asked.

Just imagine what their neighbors were thinking when they saw a huge black man in a purple suit riding a tractor in the middle of a ten-acre farm. But hell, someone needed to cut the grass so I could play some golf.

I never asked myself why what happened to me happened to me. Some people do everything in excess. That's me. Everything I do, I go full speed. It's no wonder the Giants took out an insurance policy on me when I was playing for them. A lot of people thought I wouldn't make it past my thirtieth birthday . . . and LT, the daredevil, took pride in that.

Against all odds, I've made it to forty-four. I've always thought there were angels looking out for me. I'm lucky to be alive. I lived life as if there was no tomorrow, and more than a few times there almost was no tomorrow for me.

I never kept clippings, but I see now why players do. It's not until later in life that you learn to appreciate your accomplishments. I don't know how football fans will remember me years from now, but I like what Wellington Mara said when someone asked him how he would like Giant fans to remember me. "Just a great player who never gave up," Mr. Mara said. "Never did less than his best."

BILL WALSH, 49ers Hall of Fame coach

The combination of rare physical gifts and his intensity on the field made LT one of the greatest players of all time.

He was like a Jerry Rice or a Joe Montana. He was the best at his position at his time, and maybe ever.

I appreciate it when Bill Parcells tells people that I inspired him, and inspired my teammates.

BYRON HUNT

He played every down like it was the last down he was ever going to play.

GEORGE MARTIN

If they had charged his teammates to attend games to watch him play, we gladly would have paid it.

I once told someone that I know what it is to shake hands with the devil. Hell, I know what it is to eat dinner with the devil. And get stuck with the bill.

When I was a boy, I was a church deacon. Sometimes we put religion on a back burner; sometimes we forget that God is there. Religion is for those of us who don't want to go to hell. Spirituality is for those of us who've already been there. And I've been there.

I know who I am now, finally, and I know where I'm going. My name is Lawrence Taylor and I'm an addict.

It was LT who thought he could drink and smoke cocaine and party all night and chase quarterbacks on no sleep and

leap tall buildings in a single bound. It was LT who thought he could whip the demon cocaine on the golf course. It was LT who sneered at danger. It was LT who marched to the beat of his own drummer, and thought the music would never stop.

It was Lawrence Taylor who was left alone when the music stopped.

It was Lawrence Taylor who had to get off his knees and stand on his own two feet.

It was Lawrence Taylor who had to fight for his life.

It was a humbling fall, and it has been a long, lonely struggle through emptiness, darkness, and despair, but I made it.

These days, when I hear sirens, I don't think they're coming for me. There used to be a time I'd ride by a cop scared he was gonna pull me over. I know I ain't got no license if they stop me. Now if they stop me, I pull out my license, and I don't have to worry about them running checks on me. I don't worry about those things anymore.

I used to have a phobia about being broke. I don't worry about that. I can make money doing just about anything. I'm happy. I'm not the happiest man in the world—I *am* married . . . just kidding. But I don't have the worries I used to have, many of which were self-inflicted. I created a lot of problems during the nineties for myself and hid from 'em. The littlest of problems always come back. You might not think about it, but they always come back. It took time, but all those problems have gone away.

I've been clean for five years now. I may have a beer every now and then, but absolutely no drugs. I'm not all the way to where I want to be, but when I think back to where I *was*, I'm proud. I see now that my life has kind of followed my pattern during an NFL season—I always started strong, then fell asleep a little bit, but I always came on strong in the end. I always do.

I'm Lawrence Taylor, and I'm proud of who the fuck I am.

GOING *OVER THE EDGE*:
DELETED SCENES

There were so many stories from so many of my friends, teammates, and family that we couldn't figure out a way to get them all into the book. So here are some scenes that ended up on the cutting-room floor.

BYRON HUNT,
Giants linebacker and roommate

We checked into the hotel and we hit the road. We had a designated taxi cab driver who would take us to some of the hangouts for women you would never want to be seen with but you always wanted to be with. We had the driver cut the meter off and take us anywhere we wanted to go. I will say this: we found the only go-go brothel in Green Bay, Wisconsin. This was a place that opened at five P.M. Lawrence and I were there at four-thirty. We didn't have much time; we had to be at the [Saturday night] meeting at nine o'clock.

KEVIN HELLER, pal, jeweler

One of the hottest models at the time used to hang out at the Underground with this makeup artist. The guy was fawning from afar over Lawrence. So he has the girl go over to Lawrence and ask him how big his cock was. Lawrence says, "I can't give you fifteen, but I can give you at least two eights!"

STEVE STREATER, pal, UNC teammate

After Lawrence made a tackle, and everybody was around the football, he'd always tell the other team, "Look, don't keep calling timeouts, let the clock run, you can't win, we've got to go back to the Lounge [our dorm room]. We've got a party to go to. You're all invited, but let's get the game over with!"

PHIL SIMMS, Giants quarterback

The phone rings. It's like 5:48 Sunday morning. I go, "Who in the hell is calling me this early?" He goes, "Man, are you asleep? What is it with you white people always sleeping?" I laugh and I go, "You're just coming in, aren't you big boy?" And he says, "Oh yeah. I'm driving up the highway right now. I'll be at your house in ten minutes. I want to play golf. You wanna play?" I go, "No, I'm going to church. I don't want to play golf."

Lawrence says, "I need some golf clothes. I need shoes." At 6:05, he pulls in. My wife goes out with me. He's got these really thick black leather pants on, like a gator skin. I go, "Lawrence, I don't have any pants that'll fit you." He goes, "Well give me golf shoes." I give him golf shoes, he puts them on, and goes, "What do you think?" I said, "You are changing the face of golf with this look." He's out there swinging his clubs, checking things out. I said, "I'm going back to bed." He drives down the street, there's a golf course two miles away from my house, and he played all day long.

RUSTY HAWLEY, Giants VP of marketing

From the standpoint of his specific approach to shot-making and this and that, he was very respectful of the game. He could be a little bit disrespectful toward some of the finer nuances, such as waiting for the next group to tee off. He would tee off first and occasionally he would just follow his ball right off the tee box, and the rest of us would be left to try to steer our shots around him or hopefully over him, knowing if we failed to do so, there would have been considerable consequences.

LAWRENCE TAYLOR, Author

I met my pal Dino on the golf course. We're at Spook Rock and it's the tenth hole. I'm kicking his ass and taking his money. Out of the blue, he asks me, "Aren't you afraid of catching AIDS?" I tell him, "I always carry a rubber in my bag." He says, "Really? You have one in your bag now?"

"Yeah, why?"

"I never got fucked by a big black dick. Can we go in the woods and you can fuck me in the ass?"

"What'd you say?"

"What's the big deal? No one knows."

"Are you fucked up?"

"No, I'm serious."

Motherfucker won every hole after that, and I told the starter afterward, "If you ever hook me up with a queer again I'll kill you!" And the starter says to me, "Are you kidding? He's the biggest whore in town!"

Dino and I became best friends. He used to be my Go-Get-'Em: "Hey, go get that girl right there." I'm the deal closer. He's the Go-Get-'Em.

STEVE DeOSSIE, Giants linebacker

We were stretching before practice one day. Now you have to understand, stupid shit comes up all the time. So this one day, it was me, Pepper Johnson, Banks, and LT. Someone asked, "Would you suck Michael Jackson's dick for ten million dollars?"

So we go around the group and everybody had to answer. "Hell no!" one of the guys said. "That's gross," another one said. So on and so forth. LT was last.

"What about you, Lawrence?"

So LT thinks about it, and thinks about it some more. He looks at us and says, "Ten million dollars, huh?"

"Ten million dollars, yes."

He thinks about it some more.

"Tax-free?"

DOWNTOWN JULIE BROWN,
TV personality and friend

You know how he likes to eat chicken sandwiches with the bone? Half a chicken between two pieces of bread. And a couple of vanilla shakes.

COREY MILLER, Giants linebacker

He brought this girl back to his penthouse suite in Miami, and the girl fixed him a drink. He takes a sip. He wakes up the next day and his Rolex watch is gone and all his money's gone, and he was left there naked on the bed.

ERIC "DOC" PRUDEN, a D'Fella

One night Lawrence took us to Manhattan and we were riding around New York. He said, "Come on, let me show you something." So he drove us down this street and he said, "Look down there. There's working girls down there." It couldn't have been thirty seconds later, a big police paddy wagon pulled up. And I have never seen women run so fast in high heels to this day! That was awesome.

ERIC DORSEY, Giants defensive end

George Martin told me not to mess with him, he'll take it too far. It started off real small, we were both chewing tobacco, maybe I took a can out of his locker, maybe he took a can out of mine. But I knew this particular prank LT used to pull all the time, so I used to check the rear of my truck in the parking lot. For a while, everything was fine. Then one day, I notice a sign taped over my license plate: COPS SUCK.

One morning, I had to go to treatment during training camp, like seven o'clock. When I left the dormitory to get into my truck, I saw Lawrence Taylor doing sprints and jogging on the highway that goes around the camp. And you gotta remember, if I saw him at seven, he must have been out there at six.

CHARLIE ALEXANDER,
LT's insurance agent

LT and the guys invited some ladies to a friend's house. After a while, everybody got comfortable. And one of the girls had to bring her little poodle with her. She's in the bedroom with Lawrence and starts screaming in the heat of passion. And the dog went running and bit Lawrence on the ass.

RICKY BARDEN
played defensive back at UNC

When Lawrence would give girls an autograph [at the 1986 Pro Bowl], he'd write our room number on there. It was sex every night, from Tuesday to Sunday. Sometimes you had two of 'em at a time, out on the balcony, 'cause you know in Hawaii how the weather is. You got two women out there doing whatever to you. The next day, he'd be at our room early wanting to know what happened. I was like, "I wish you could have been there, but I'm glad you weren't." LT's greedy. He'll try to take over everything.

I used to go to his New Year's Eve parties. Eddie Murphy was living in Upper Saddle River, too. Eddie sent five or six girls over to Lawrence's party one time, and when they got there, they had a message from Eddie: "You all are at the wrong party!" Lawrence looked at them and said, "Man, by the looks of things, maybe we are at the wrong party!"

MARK BAVARO, Giants tight end

One time this rookie thought Lawrence had baby-powdered his locker, and he returned the favor. The rookie was mistaken. When Lawrence sees his locker, the kid's looking at him like, "That's payback!" The next thing you know, all the kid's stuff in his locker is on the bathroom floor, and it's on fire.

KEITH BYARS, Eagles running back

He has a good short game. But this one time, one hundred yards from the seventh hole at Mizner Country Club in Boca, he hit a sand wedge all of forty yards. You know how Bo Jackson would sometimes break his baseball bat over his knee? That's what LT did with his golf club. We get to nine and he goes in the pro shop and says, "Give me another club."

JOHN "J.D." MORNING

We [D'Fellas] went to the playoff game in Philadelphia his rookie year. He didn't even ride back in the [team] bus. He drove my car back, a 1977 Dodge Colt, so all of us could ride together.

KEITH BYARS

The first two times, I got pretty good cut-blocks on him. Then the only drive we mounted all day, we had first-and-goal at the five-yard line. I went to cut him, and as soon as I dove into his legs, he turned into Superman. He jumped right over me, drilled Ron Jaworski right in the back, and caused a fumble. I was on the bench the rest of the day.

RONNIE LOTT, 49ers Hall of Fame safety

He always sings a song about New York, and the song he sings is the same lyrics and the same tune as Mickey Mouse. Every time I see him I request that song. It goes something like: "Who's the great-est in N-Y-C . . . LT . . . LT . . . Why? Because he loves you!" For me, that song represents his love for New York, his love for the Giants, his love for playing the game of football, man. His love for trying to be the best.

CHRIS MARA, Giants executive

We were on our way to San Francisco, I believe. He used to play golf on Monday, the day of the game. They had told him they didn't want him playing. He walked on the plane and he had his golf clubs under his mink overcoat so George Young and Parcells couldn't see them.

BOB DRURY,
New York Post beat writer in 1981

I'm with LT, Beasley Reece, and Billy Taylor in training camp. We all start drinking shots of kamikazes, which was big at the time. LT says, "Shots are for pussies," and he orders a pitcher of kamikazes and chugs it, and slides headfirst down the bar. He took a running leap and threw himself up on the corner of the bar and slid for about five feet, and then stood up and said: "Okay, who's ready to go to Manhattan?"

RUSS FABER, sports agent

I had a seven A.M. tee time with LT one time. He said he met a waitress at a bar in the Orlando area. Typical LT: He takes her home. He said, "You know, when I first met her, I didn't really like her 'cause she smoked a lot." The next morning, he was at a 7-Eleven buying her a pack of cigarettes.

BRAD VAN PELT, Giants linebacker

We were at the Front Row, it's about two in the morning, music's blaring, and everybody's dancing. He walks over to me, puts his arm around me matter-of-factly, and asks, "What are you doing?"

"I'm dancing."

He looks at me incredulously and says: "No you're not. At least you're not dancing to the same music I'm dancing to."

BOB PUTT, General Manager of LT's

The grand opening [of LT's] was an event. We had the Hawthorne Caballeros lined up in front of the restaurant. Traffic was backed up along Route 17. Lawrence took one of the sabres of one of the Hawthorne Caballero people there and was standing on the roof waving the sabre, dressed in a tuxedo.

LAWRENCE TAYLOR

Me and some friends went on a golf trip to Boca, and I met this schoolteacher there, a nice girl. The next night I'm gonna take this girl to dinner. Well, she came over and she accompanies me back into the back room, and never got her dinner. My friend Gary and his friends had gone out to dinner. I ordered Domino's pizza. And when they came back late, I knew they were gonna be hungry. So I put the Domino's pizza right on the table, right? And I took this girl's panties and put them inside the pizza box. I hear them, "Oh, we got Domino's!"

One of the guys was with a girl he had just met. You know, he's trying to be all proper, "Oh, eat some pizza," and stuff. They open that bad boy . . . oh man, to see the look on his face.

BUDDY CURRY,
UNC and Falcons linebacker

We went to a fraternity party during summer school and they had a keg. I brought Lawrence. Lawrence took the keg and carried it into our room; I think we were on the second or third floor. We were going to have a little party there. The fraternity guys came over and asked, "Mr. Taylor, could we please have our keg back?"

MATT VASGERSIAN, *Toughman* announcer

A lot of his humor was racially charged humor, but it was always self-deprecating. If you're white, you're blue, you're yellow—you're going to laugh. It was closing time and everybody was filtering out. The fiancé of a buxom ring-card girl in the stands had just won one of the Toughman titles and was being awarded the belt inside the ring. She's bouncing up and down; all you can see is breast meat moving around. He points to the screen with his finger, and in the background of the shot you see three black guys. She's still on the periphery of the ring. He says, "Looky here, the brothers are starting to circle up."

PETER KING,
Sports Illustrated football writer

It's 12:15 A.M., preseason finale in 1988, the fog rolling in off Lake Erie. [Browns coach Marty] Schottenheimer puts [quarterback] Bernie [Kosar] back in with three minutes to go. The Browns are up 17–13. I'm on the field. I look over and there's LT grabbing a helmet on the ground and running onto the field yelling, "Andy, Andy." Taylor says to Andy Headen, "Head man sent me in." Belichick is on the field screaming at Taylor, "Get out of there, get out of there!" Headen has to run to the sidelines. Taylor ramrods the middle to stop some big back from scoring. After the game, I say to him, "God, meaningless game." He said, "Hey, we got our pride. I'm not gonna let a team embarrass us."

PROPS

Here's some nice shit some great people have said about me. For the record, this was not my idea, but my editor's.

MIKE DITKA, former Bears and Saints coach   He had great athletic ability and great instincts, which are good to have, but I always thought he wanted to be the best. I can remember the first time I saw him (as an aide to the late Cowboys legend Tom Landry). I went in to Coach Landry and said, "You see this number 56 guy with the Giants?" And he said, "Yeah, he's quite a football player. I don't know how we're gonna block him." Coming from him, that was the ultimate compliment.

JOHN ELWAY, former Broncos quarterback   He is one of the all-time great linebackers in the NFL. He revolutionized the game by being a stand-up linebacker who rushed the passer. His great athleticism and tenacity made him one of the best of all time.

JOE MONTANA, former 49ers quarterback　He's gotta be the best that played that position. He could do everything, in my mind.

JERRY RICE, Raiders receiver　The most physical player on the football field. I'm talking about speed, I'm talking about technique—he brought everything to the table. And his presence out there was very intimidating because as a quarterback you knew that this guy, nobody could block him, and that he was gonna be back there in the backfield and he was gonna make plays and he was gonna intimidate. He was the best. The best to ever play the game.

ERIC DICKERSON, former Colts running back　He gave it all he had, all the time. That's the way you're supposed to play the sport you love. He made you fear him. I don't think you'll find a guy more feared and who could play in any era. That's how I look at players. He could play right now, he could play ten years ago, he could play twenty years ago, he could play fifteen years from now. He could do it all. It's hard to intimidate players. But he had that intimidation factor; he'd hit you and then talk to you—"It's gonna be like that all day long; you can't run over here; you can't do that to me, I'm LT." That intimidates a lot of players if you don't have a strong heart. He did it week after week, year after year.

EMMITT SMITH, all-time rushing leader　He was awesome. He was still making plays when I came into the league [1990]. Not only do I keep my mind on him, the whole offense keeps their mind on him, too.

DICK BUTKUS, former Bears middle linebacker I'd say that he made the corner linebacker an impact position where before it was middle linebacker.

BILL BELICHICK, Patriots coach and former Giants assistant I wasn't in the league when Dick Butkus played, but I don't see how you could put anybody above him [LT]. He could play as a defensive lineman and he did everything you'd want a linebacker to do exceptionally well, and was bigger and faster and stronger than all of them. He did everything you could do with a high level of aggressiveness—*consistently*. Maybe there was someone better, but I can't imagine someone with more talent, toughness, football instinctiveness, over the ten years I coached him.

DEREK JETER, Yankee shortstop What stands out for me was he was better than everybody else. I think everyone feared him. When he's on defense, you try to find him. I think a lot of people try to follow the offensive side of the ball, you know, watch the quarterback. But I always found myself trying to find him, see what he's doing.

MIKE PIAZZA, Mets catcher He played the game like a tiger. Didn't leave anything on the field. Just completely dominated the position.

KAREEM ABDUL-JABBAR, Hall of Fame basketball legend I was a Giants fan as a kid. I used to watch them at Yankee Stadium. I wore number 33 because of Mel Triplett. He [LT] really brought so much fire and physical talent and just a desire to prevail. He was like a primal force out there. He was really awesome to watch. He was something else.

JOE THEISMANN, former Redskins quarterback
The greatest outside linebacker who ever played the game of professional football. The best way to describe how we as a football team felt about Lawrence Taylor was when the team sits down in a team meeting, they put little *Xs* and *Os* on the board to designate offense and defense, *S* for safety, and so on. Lawrence was the only person whose number we put up.

RON JAWORSKI, former Eagles quarterback   In my opinion, he was the greatest linebacker ever to play the game, and maybe the greatest defender ever to play the game.

DAN REEVES, Falcons coach   He changed the way you had to block a 3-4 defense. Everybody started trying to find Lawrence Taylors.

RANDALL CUNNINGHAM, former Eagles quarterback
There was no one better. When he put his uniform on, he was Robocop.

RANDY CROSS, former 49ers center   He was to his position what Jerry Rice is to wide receiver, what Mike Vick may be to quarterback, what Barry [Sanders] was to halfback.

WARREN MOON, former Oilers quarterback   He played the game with an attitude. He played like he had a chip on his shoulder. He wanted to be dominant all the time, and he wanted the people around him to be dominant. He made the other guys around him play at another level that they wouldn't normally play at. I would think he's probably the most dominating single defensive player to ever play the game. He was just a guy that you always had to account for when you played against him.

STEVE BARTKOWSKI, former Falcons quarterback
He was *the* most incredible football player I've ever been on the field with. Nobody changed the face of the NFL more than he did. He had the rare combination of size and speed, and when you throw in with that the tenacity he had, you had the prototypical superstar. That's just who he was. He had great instincts; he had everything the great ones have . . . the ability to seize the moment. When a play needed to be made . . . not unlike a Deion Sanders or a John Elway . . . that sort of charisma, to rise up at just the right time and make the play the game sorta turns on.

MARV ALBERT, legendary broadcaster   When you think of Lawrence Taylor, you think of guys who not only changed the game, but became so identifiable with defense. He'd show up at practice and play stops, and the other players would gawk. Very few athletes would get that reaction.

JOE JACOBY, former Redskins left tackle   He revolutionized that position. You look at all the players now trying to be like him. Like in the National Basketball Association, everybody's trying to be Like Mike.

JOHNIE COOKS, former Colts and Giants linebacker
Eric Dickerson is my favorite running back. But LT was the best football player to ever play.

DONNELL THOMPSON, former LT teammate at North Carolina and Colts defensive tackle   Every year you hear someone come out and say, "That's The Next LT." I haven't seen The Next LT yet. He was special. I haven't seen any man put on a football uniform that plays defense like I've seen LT play defense. He is The Best, bar none. He is the best defensive player to ever play the game of football in the history of the National Football League.

MARV LEVY, former Bills coach   He was one of those guys that we used to look at on film and Bill Polian, our general manager, would turn to me and say, "Why don't they all do it like that?" When you start saying, "Who was the greatest linebacker?" you're gonna hear Butkus, you're gonna hear . . . I've always said who was the greatest what at any position is almost an injustice to six or seven other guys right there, but he's one of those six or seven, I'll tell you that.

ROMEO CRENNEL, former Giants assistant   He played the game on the edge and he was gonna give it everything he had, and he expected everybody around him to give it all they had. He could will things to happen. He is one of those players that changed the game.

LAMAR LEACHMAN, former Giants assistant   Probably during Lawrence's day, he was probably the best linebacker that ever walked on the field.

DAVE MEGGETT, former Giants running back   If he played the middle, he probably would have been the best middle linebacker. If he played the strong side, he probably would have been the best strong side linebacker. In all honesty, wherever he would have played, he probably would have been the best.

JON BON JOVI, musical performer I loved that he had eyes all over the field. He's up there certainly with the greats of all time. I'm glad that he made the Hall of Fame. I'm glad that it seems his personal problems are behind him. He's a legend's legend.

DON KING, boxing promoter Lawrence Taylor was one of the best defensive players that I've ever seen. He was a giant. And he *was* a Giant. He was a giant in manhood and he was a giant in playing for the Giants. I liked his character and his never-say-die attitude. He had a will to win. That was so remarkable for me, to find a man with handicaps and he would have his problems and his setbacks, but when he'd go on that football field he was superb. And I've always respected him for that in doing his job and doing it to the best of his ability. So I love LT.

LARRY HOLMES, former heavyweight champion I liked his toughness, his roughness, his arrogance on the field. I don't really know him personally, but him and Mark Gastineau were my two favorite players out there. He [LT] played with a lot of intensity.

RICKY WATTERS, former 49ers running back The things I remember are like him just like coming, play after play, game after game. I mean, he's just coming. And he's not stopping. And even in the twilight of his career, he was still that way. He was still coming, he was still letting you know he's there.

MICHAEL IRVIN, former Cowboys receiver LT reinvented the game. The way we play the game. People talk about the way he played the game. The same thing I tell Terrell Owens today. He plays with such enthusiasm, and he enjoys the game. I said, "People all talk about you, but they'll remember you for it." So that's what LT did. There were very few guys ever played the game that controlled the whole football game from the defensive position. He did.

LYNN SWANN, former Steelers receiver   He was an impact player on the highest order. When offenses are changing their blocking schemes for what you do, and you're *still* having success.

PAUL ZIMMERMAN, *Sports Illustrated*   Lawrence Taylor is the greatest at a unique position, and that position is called rush linebacker, which is a new position that he created. You can't call him a linebacker because he didn't have a linebacker's responsibilities. His basic role was as a down edge rusher, a specialist, who played an occasional linebacker. Once every two years, he'd have a coverage responsibility. But as an edge rusher, he's the greatest who ever lived.

PETER KING, *Sports Illustrated*   Guys say they play every game like it's their last game. Lawrence Taylor felt it would have been an honorable death to die on the football field. Because that's what he did. That was his job. I just feel he is Russell Crowe in *Gladiator*. He's the guy who, more than any other player I've ever seen, so many times willed himself when he had no business being out there. When he played with that torn pectoral muscle in New Orleans, that was easily the most heroic performance I'd ever seen. I think he was a great player who played at a high level. He probably could have been greater if he could have tamed himself in his personal life. But then he wouldn't have been LT.

JOHNNIE COCHRAN, attorney   He had such passion for the game. He was probably in the tradition of guys like Jack Lambert, the guys who were the passionate linebackers. He was a new modern type of linebacker, which I thought was just great, and I love him.

STACY ROBINSON, former Giants receiver   I think LT was The Ultimate Defensive Weapon.

PAT SUMMERALL, ex-Giant and television broadcaster   He was as good as there has ever been at that position, and I've seen a lot of them. He'd be in the top five players of all time in Giant history, and I wouldn't be surprised if you couldn't say that about NFL history, too.

ERIC DORSEY, former Giants defensive end   The man changed the game. People are still looking for The Next LT.

CURTIS MARTIN, Jets running back   I just remember that he was relentless. To me, he was like the epitome of what a football player was as far as mentally tough, physically tough; probably one of the greatest ever to play defense, if not the greatest.

WILLIS REED, former Knicks captain   I think that one thing Lawrence Taylor had is that he had that ability to come every Sunday or Monday and play at a high level. His pursuit on the field was unbelievable. He could actually get knocked down, get up, and go all the way across the field and make the tackle, which was the most unbelievable thing. I just thought he had a great will to win and a great desire and determination. That's what made him a special athlete.

BRUCE HARPER, Jets running back and return specialist   He's the best linebacker, certainly. I would even go as far as saying the best defensive player ever to play football. He played fair, that's first. He just gave it all up, completely. He was fast, he hit hard, he was strong, he was smart . . . he was ready to play football. He *was* football.

JOHN FRANCO, Mets reliever   You never saw him not give 100 percent. On every play, he was out there busting his tail and had the attitude that he felt like somebody was trying to take food off the table from him. He went out there and attacked and attacked and attacked until he got the job done.

KEITH BYARS, former Eagles running back   He was the total package. It's almost a disservice to him when they compare a lot of players to him. I could study all the film I wanted and couldn't ever figure out any tendencies, like the perfect way to block him. I always slept a lot easier on Saturday night the other fourteen weeks of the year when we didn't have to play the Giants.

CAREER STATS

Season	Team	Games	Sacks	INT	Int/Yds	Avg	TD	Fumbles
1981	NYG	16	n/a	1	1	1.0	0	1
1982	NYG	9	7.5	1	97	97	1	0
1983	NYG	16	9.0	2	10	5.0	0	1
1984	NYG	16	11.5	1	−1	−1.0	0	0
1985	NYG	16	13.0	0	0	0.0	0	0
1986	NYG	16	20.5	0	0	0.0	0	0
1987	NYG	12	12.0	3	16	5.3	0	0
1988	NYG	12	15.5	0	0	0.0	0	0
1989	NYG	16	15.0	0	0	0.0	0	0
1990	NYG	16	10.5	1	11	11.0	1	0
1991	NYG	14	7.0	0	0	0.0	0	0
1992	NYG	9	5.0	0	0	0.0	0	0
1993	NYG	16	6.0	0	0	0.0	0	0
Career		184	132	9	134	14.9	2	2